THE GOLDEN
OF
NORTHUMBRIA

by
Jane Hawkes

fig.1 - Anglo-Saxon 'inhabited vine scroll' sculpture, from Jarrow Monastery, Tyne and Wear.
St. Paul's Church, Jarrow.

Contents

onginneð   godspelles

incipit euangelii

hic   genelogia mathei

LIB ER

GENERATI

ONISIHU

XPIFILIIDAUIDFILIIABRAHAM

Foreword

Tyne & Wear Museums is delighted to have been able to collaborate with Sandhill Press on the production of this book, which is published to accompany our once-in-a-lifetime exhibition, *Treasures from the Lost Kingdom of Northumbria*. Together they celebrate the achievements of the Anglo-Saxon kingdom of Northumbria, which grew to encompass much of northern England and southern Scotland. So important is the theme of the exhibition that it deserves to have this lasting record, not only for the benefit of local visitors to the exhibition, but for an even wider audience within our region and beyond.

We have also been delighted by the generosity of the many lenders, amongst whom we must thank in particular the British Library and the British Museum. Their staff, especially Janet Backhouse and Leslie Webster, have been extremely helpful and supportive. Our thanks also to Professors Richard Bailey and Rosemary Cramp for their encouragement and advice, which has guided us from the exhibition's early days. We are most grateful to Northern Rock, Procter & Gamble, Securex Displays, the University of Northumbria at Newcastle, Tyne & Wear Museums 1996 Corporate Patrons Scheme, Friends of the Laing Art Gallery, the 'Pairing Scheme' administered by ABSA (Association for Business Sponsorship of the Arts), the Sponsors' Club, the John Ellerman Foundation and the Heritage Lottery Fund for their financial support. Finally, our thanks to our staff, especially Clive Hart, Juliet Horsley and Nick Dolan for working so effectively to bring together this extraordinary exhibition.

Councillor Don Price
Chairman, Tyne & Wear Joint Museums Committee

Dr David Fleming
Director, Tyne & Wear Museums

AUTHOR'S ACKNOWLEDGEMENTS

Thanks are due to Janet Backhouse, Leslie Webster, Clive Hart, Juliet Horsley and Mel Twelves for their time and help in the production of this book. A special thanks goes to Jason Hawkes.

fig.2 - The initial page of the Gospel of St Matthew, Lindisfarne Gospels, written at Lindisfarne, Holy Island, Northumberland in about 698; MS Cotton Nero D. iv, f.27. *British Library.*

Preface

Northumbria has a unique place in English cultural history. Poised on the borderline between two powerful cultural traditions - Roman and Celtic - and with the crucial catalyst of Anglo-Saxon political power, it became one of the greatest intellectual centres and perhaps the most dynamic powerhouse of artistic creation in the early medieval world. During the 'Golden Age' of the 7th and 8th centuries, a combination of political pre-eminence and religious transformation gave rise to something quite exceptional in the history of English art and culture. Its influence pervaded Europe for several centuries and continues to this day to colour our own national artistic awareness and cultural vocabulary.

In celebration of this momentous achievement, the exhibition *Treasures from the Lost Kingdom of Northumbria* brings together many of the greatest surviving treasures of the period, some of them returning to the region where they originated for the first time in more than a thousand years. The Lindisfarne Gospels, paramount icon of this 'Golden Age', which was removed from the Holy Island of Lindisfarne in 875 to escape the threat posed by the invading Danes, is probably travelling north of the Tyne for the first time since the shrine of St Cuthbert was established at Chester-le-Street in 883. That most enigmatic of objects, the so-called Franks Casket, may be making a similarly historic return. Through these, and other world-famous items, some glimpse may be had of the extraordinary genius that was - indeed is - peculiarly Northumbrian. This is a great and abiding culture and here it is given an appropriate celebration.

Janet Backhouse
Curator of Illuminated Manuscripts, British Library

Leslie Webster
Deputy Keeper of Medieval and Later Antiquities, British Museum

fig.3 - The Anglo-Saxon stone cross at Bewcastle, Cumbria. Viewed from the south-east.

fig.4 - Map of Anglo-Saxon England.

I

INTRODUCTION

The Kingdom of Northumbria

The term 'Northumbria' first appears in written records in the early eighth century when it is used to refer to a kingdom which extended from the Humber and Mersey in the south, to the Forth and Clyde in the north. At times the regions beyond these borders, modern-day Tayside, Humberside and northern Lincolnshire, also formed part of the territory as the Anglo-Saxon kings of Northumbria controlled events in these regions, even if they were not the direct rulers (*fig.4*).

The 'Golden Age'

During this period of political supremacy Northumbria enjoyed a sense of relative stability. The turmoil of the preceding centuries, which had seen the collapse of Roman rule in Britain during the early fifth century, followed by the upheavals of migration, conflict and settlement involving peoples from the north, east and west, had come to an end. For some 150 years, between the seventh and eighth centuries, successive rulers managed to maintain a certain equilibrium, providing the necessary economic and social conditions in which the arts (definitive of 'The Golden Age') could flourish.

Equally important to this climate of peace, prosperity and artistic outpouring was the position of the Christian Church. From the fourth decade of the seventh century it was protected and patronised by the rulers of Northumbria, ensuring its establishment as a second source of wealth and unifying power in the kingdom. Under its influence diplomatic links with the wider European world were reinforced and Northumbria was introduced to the culture of societies as diverse and widely separated as those of Ireland and the Mediterranean. It was these contacts that provided the Anglo-Saxon artists with sources of inspiration which they could fuse with their own traditions in their works of art.

fig.5 - King David as Warrior, from Cassiodorus, Commentary on the Psalms, MS B. II. 30, f.172b. Second quarter of the 8th century.
Durham Cathedral Library.

Northumbria's Influences

This was not simply a one-way process, however, with the northern artists receiving their inspiration from outside the area; the influence of Northumbrian writers and artists was also felt elsewhere. It was the work of churchmen, builders and artists from Northumbria that influenced the conversion and cultural development of Scotland and the English Midlands (Mercia) during the seventh and eighth centuries. Christian missionaries from Northumbria also went to convert the Germanic tribes of northern Europe. And, it was to Northumbria that rulers of mainland Europe sent for books and men to help reform their Churches. Between the seventh and ninth centuries, the impact of Northumbrian culture was felt far and wide.

fig.6 - Late Saxon walrus ivory pen case, showing Northumbrian influence.
British Museum.

II

SETTING THE SCENE: 'BRITANNIA INFERIOR'

Within the Roman World

The territory covered by the Anglo-Saxon kingdom of Northumbria did not emerge out of a vacuum. Before the Anglo-Saxons moved into the region it was, like much of mainland Britain, part of the Roman Empire. Indeed, referred to as 'Britannia Inferior', it had the unique distinction of being the northern-most frontier of that Empire, a fact still visible in the remains of Hadrian's Wall (*fig.7*).

The 'frontier-land' aspect of the region was a determining element in its development, both during the period of Roman occupation and in subsequent centuries. Under the Romans it meant that the British tribes living immediately north of the Wall were sustained by the army to provide a permanent 'buffer zone'; south of the Wall, it meant the military forces maintained an all-powerful presence. As a result, civilian settlements remained comparatively under-developed: there were fewer 'cities', urban communities with self-governing rights, than in lowland Britain ('Britannia Superior'). More common were mercantile settlements which were initially established close to river crossings and the major forts to cater for the needs of the military units based there. As soldiers retired from the army and settled on land granted to them in the region, these settlements grew into small towns surrounded by country estates. But, although these became prosperous places of some considerable size, they were in no way comparable with the thriving towns and cities found elsewhere.

The inhabitants of these northern communities were, according to the tombstones recording their deaths, drawn from all over the Empire: from North

fig.7 - A View of Hadrian's Wall, from Walltown Crags looking west, Cumbria.

fig.8 -
Romano-British
mosaic from
Brantingham,
Humberside,
showing a female
bust; probably 4th
century.

*Hull and East Riding
Museum.*

Africa, Syria, Italy, Germany and Spain. In their adopted homeland they married and lived amongst the Britons who, like any people conquered by the Romans, were encouraged to adopt the life-style of Roman citizens. For those who did, life had much to offer. Foodstuffs, wine and fine tableware, glass and high-quality pottery were available, often imported from the far corners of the Empire. The houses of the more affluent citizens could be centrally-heated, well-lit by oil lamps, and decorated with brightly painted plaster walls and floors covered with mosaics produced by local workshops.

At Aldborough, in North Yorkshire, there was a workshop that specialised in mosaics made up of geometric patterns; it supplied customers further afield, in Well and Winterton. Another Aldborough workshop, whose products survive at Brantingham (*fig.8*), Rudston and Horkstow on Humberside, specialised in extremely ornate mosaics depicting figural subjects: charioteers with their laurel wreath of victory, characters from classical mythology, such as Venus and Orpheus, and personified deities of rivers and the four seasons.

The Religions of the Roman North

Not only did the people of northern Britain have access to the cultural amenities of the Empire, they were also party to its religious beliefs. As was the case throughout the Roman world, numerous deities were venerated, some well known, others more obscure, even to those who worshipped them. At Catterick, for instance, an ageing soldier entrusted with tax-collecting, raised an altar dedicated to the god, unknown to him, whom he credited with having invented roads.

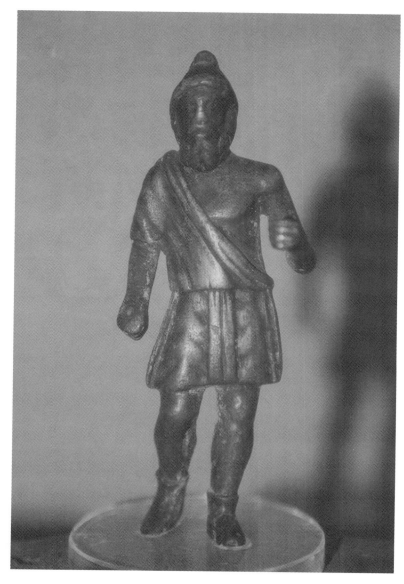

fig.9 - Bronze figurine of a Romano-British deity from Fulwell, Tyne & Wear; 2nd-3rd century.

Museum of Antiquities, University of Newcastle upon Tyne.

More common objects of devotion were the Emperor and the major state gods of Rome: Jupiter, Juno and Minerva; statues and figurines of these deities, along with altars dedicated to them, have survived from nearly every fort and settlement in the region. Given the predominantly military nature of the region, Mars, the god of war was popular, as was Mithras, a Persian god whose exclusively male devotees were drawn from the élite of the army. And, there were cults dedicated to lesser deities: Hercules and Victory were venerated at Birdoswald, Chesters and South Shields; Neptune and Oceanus guarded the bridge across the River Tyne at Newcastle; a crowned 'genius loci' (the spirit of a given place), protected the town of Carlisle.

fig.10 - Early Christian Romano-British 'Chi-Rho' inscribed tile from York; 4th century.

York Minster Foundations and Treasury.

It was as one of these religious cults that Christianity was first introduced to Britain during the late second century; by the fourth century it was well-established. In 314, the year after Christianity was granted official toleration throughout the Empire, three British bishops attended a Council at Arles; one of these was the Bishop of York. His presence suggests that by this time the Church in the North was a highly structured organisation with dioceses and parishes served by a hierarchy of clergymen.

There is, however, no recognisable trace of the buildings used by these early northern Christians; there are no signs of the churches such as those which have survived in lowland Britain at Silchester (Hampshire), for example. Our knowledge of Christianity in the Roman North thus depends on a few isolated objects recovered from burials and building rubble: some Christian artefacts included in a fourth-century burial at York, and a Christian tombstone recovered from the Roman cemetery at Harraby (Carlisle); a table altar from South Shields; and a small sandstone block from Catterick and a tile from York (*fig.10*), both decorated with the chi-rho symbol (the letters *X* and *P*, the initial letters of the word 'Christ' in Greek).

Alongside Christianity and the other cults imported by the Romans, the religious traditions of the Celtic British population also continued to flourish. Their survival is demonstrated by objects such as the stone 'severed heads' from Corbridge (*fig.11*) and Ilkley, or stone reliefs carved with images of hooded 'dwarves' and 'mother-goddesses'. The survival of many of these reliefs at military forts (such as Housesteads), demonstrates that these local British-Celtic cults were often observed among those serving in the Roman army.

fig.11 - Romano-British stone 'severed' head, from Corbridge, Northumberland.
Corbridge Museum.

A spring at Carrawburgh (on Hadrian's Wall), for instance, had long been the site of a British shrine. In the second century it was embellished with a number of Roman carvings, one of which depicts a naturalistically reclining woman identified by an inscription as 'Coventina'. Here, something that may have been no more than a vague notion of sanctity among the local population was transformed by the Romans into a recognisable deity. The Roman appropriation of British religious cults also produced some strange anomalies. While the Britons did not always name their deities, the Romans did; at Benwell the result was an altar raised to 'three witches' in an attempt to endow a local shrine with the paraphernalia deemed necessary for proper veneration.

The Art of the Romano-British

The art produced under such conditions in northern Britain was evidently open to many influences, the most prominent being the very different artistic traditions of the Roman Empire and the native Britons.

As part of the classical Mediterranean world, Roman art was based on naturalistic representations of human figures, plants and animals. The mosaics,

fig.12 - The Roman silver 'lanx' (tray) from Corbridge, Northumberland; 4th century.
British Museum.

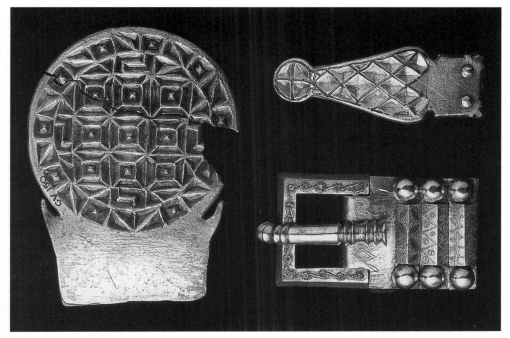

fig.13 - 4th-century buckle and strap-ends from the hoard buried in the late 4th or early 5th century at Traprain Law, Lothian, showing the 'chip-carving' technique and geometric designs employed by Germanic craftsmen.

National Museum of Scotland.

wall paintings, pottery and metalwork illustrate men and women, gods and mythical creatures sometimes set in idealised landscapes. A magnificent, imported silver 'lanx' (large platter or tray) found at Corbridge (*fig.12*) is decorated with a number of male and female deities dressed in robes and tunics standing by a temple conversing with each other. The scene may represent the ancient shrine of Apollo on the Greek island of Delos.

Apart from their own art, the Romans brought with them into the region the artistic traditions of other cultures. The Germanic peoples who served in the army wore military accoutrements made and decorated by their own metalworkers using techniques traditional to their culture. By a method known as 'chip carving', a design would be carved into the model used to make the mould, reproducing the effect of carved wood when the object was cast. Items found among a hoard of Romano-British silver buried at Traprain Law (Lothian), include pieces cast in this way: bold geometric patterns whose sharp, deeply cut angular lines emphasise the effect of light hitting their surfaces (*fig.13*).

Alongside work such as this was the art of the native Celtic Britons. It was an art based primarily on curvilinear patterns. Spiralling trumpet motifs cover the surface of the metalwork and jewellery (like the brooch from Greatchesters)

fig.14 - Romano-British relief of a woman, from Bewcastle, Cumbria, carved in the stylised patterning of local manufacture; 2nd or 3rd century.

Tullie House Museum and Art Gallery, Carlisle.

fig.15 - The 'Aesica' brooch from Greatchesters, on Hadrian's Wall, Northumberland, late 1st or 2nd century.

Museum of Antiquities, University of Newcastle upon Tyne.

fig.16 - Open-work Roman bronze 'triskele' mount composed of confronted, Celtic-style, trumpet patterns, from the Roman fort at South Shields, Tyne & Wear; 2nd century.

Museum of Antiquities, University of Newcastle upon Tyne.

produced by local craftsmen. These are the hall-marks of an artistic tradition based on notions of space, line and form, not realistic representations.

Of course, in the multi-ethnic society of Roman Britain these diverse artistic traditions also served as sources of mutual inspiration, resulting, not simply in the designs of one tradition being used to decorate objects associated with another (as with the 'Germanic' Roman military equipment), but in the development of new art styles incorporating features from all the various traditions. Contained in the trumpet patterns of the Greatchesters brooch (*fig.15*), for instance, are a pair of very stylised sea-horses, or dolphins - creatures which were introduced from a Roman repertoire of decorative animal motifs.

Alternatively, inspired by Celtic traditions, the Romans developed a taste for openwork spiralling 'triskele' mounts, composed of three pairs of confronted trumpet patterns (*fig.16*). And, under the influence of native art, the naturalistic forms of human figures in the Roman art of Britain demonstrate a strong interest in line and pattern. The commemorative portrait of a woman carved on a relief from Bewcastle depicts the figure as a series of large sweeping concentric curves which represent, stylistically, the robe covering the arms, legs and torso (*fig.14*).

III

THE COMING OF THE ANGLO - SAXONS

People on the Move

The transition from Roman Britain to Anglo-Saxon England is perhaps the least well understood period in the history of the British Isles. By the fifth century the military and economic structures upholding the Roman Empire and its material culture were disintegrating. For decades it had been weakened by revolts and challenges to the imperial throne; there was even one made by a British claimant, Constantine III (406-411). At the same time the imperial provinces were being subjected to constant attacks by armies of Germanic warriors. In an attempt to contain this situation the Roman army was recalled from Britannia, and despite pleas for their return, the Romano-British population was left without protected access to the fast-disappearing trade networks of the Empire, and without military support in the face of raids on their own territories.

For generations, people from the highlands of Scotland, referred to by Roman writers as 'Picts' (painted people), had raided the tribal lands of the Votadini and Selgovae, those who had formed the 'buffer-zone' north of Hadrian's Wall. In the fifth century, without the Roman army to sustain the balance of power in the area, these attacks increased in number and intensity, forcing the satellite tribes to move south. From Ireland came raiding parties of 'Scots', one of which captured and enslaved a young Briton known as 'Patrick' who would subsequently play an important role in consolidating the Christian Church in Ireland. And from the east came the 'Anglo-Saxons'.

fig.17 - Carved wood prow of vessel, probably 5th century, found in the River Scheldt, Appels, Belgium.
British Museum.

Barbarians from the East

fig.18 - Anglo-Saxon male inhumation burial from Norton, Cleveland.

According to the tradition preserved most effectively by Bede (the early eighth-century historian of the English Church), the Anglo-Saxons came to Britain in the mid fifth century, invited by the leaders of the Romanised Britons, who sought their protection against the raids of the Picts and the Scots. Unfortunately, it was, according to Bede, a particularly treacherous crew which took up this call to arms, for no sooner had they arrived and accepted their pay and the land allotted them, than they proceeded to form an alliance with the very people they had been hired to fight.

In a particularly vivid passage of his *Ecclesiastical History* (I, 15) Bede describes the almost total annihilation of the British population resulting from the alliance: the island was torched; buildings were destroyed; people were slain, sometimes "in heaps" leaving none to bury the dead. Those who did survive were condemned to slavery, exile, or eking out an existence in the wilderness. It was only the chance survival of Romanised aristocrats such as Ambrosius Aurelianus (sometimes identified by later generations as King Arthur), who managed to stem this tide of 'ethnic cleansing'. Under his leadership the Britons fought back, and after winning a battle at Badon Hill established a period of peace that lasted for some forty years.

For all the colour and emotive language of this account, however, the arrival of the Anglo-Saxons was probably not quite as cataclysmic an event as Bede's description would lead us to believe. From the archaeological record it is clear that life did change dramatically during the fifth century for those living in the more urbanised Roman communities. However, Bede's picture of an apocalyptic sweep of barbarian hordes across the island, driving the local population inexorably before them, to be stopped only by the heroic efforts of one legendary leader, probably owes more to Latin and Biblical literary traditions than historical reality. For, while Bede may well have been right about who it was who replaced the Romano-Britons as the dominant ethnic group living in England, how this change took place is less clear.

fig.19 -
Glass
claw beaker,
from
Castle Eden,
Co.Durham;
a luxury item or
heirloom brought
into the region from the
Rhineland by the earliest
Anglo-Saxon settlers;
5th century.
British Museum.

Certainly, as Bede claims, it would appear that significant numbers of people from northern Germany, Denmark, the Netherlands and southern Scandinavia came to live in 'England' during the fifth century. Archaeological evidence shows that inhumation (burial of the body) was the main funerary practice in Roman Britain by the fourth century, but during the fifth century a very different form of burial was introduced: cremation, when the body was burnt and the remains placed in a handmade, often decorated, clay pot, before being buried, sometimes with a number of personal possessions. This distinctive funerary practice, as well as the types of pots and possessions buried with the dead, are all closely matched in cemeteries of fourth and fifth-century date in those areas of continental Europe identified by Bede as the ancestral homelands of the Anglo-Saxons.

In Northumbria the cemetery evidence indicates that the initial Germanic migration was concentrated in the area south of the Tees. Here, in Teeside, North Yorkshire and Humberside, cremation formed the predominant funerary rite, while north of the Tees funerary practices were more varied, with inhumation continuing to be practiced alongside cremation (fig.18).

How these peoples came to settle in Northumbria (and England as a whole), is still far from clear, but the burials in the early Anglo-Saxon cemeteries do indicate that Britain was unlikely to have been overrun by a few boat-loads of mutinous Germanic mercenaries, as Bede claims. The remains are those of men, women and children, and their personal possessions include, not only the weapons of the men, but also the jewellery worn by women (fig.20). In addition there are imported luxury items, such as a glass bowl found in York, which was made in the Meuse region of Germany, or a strangely shaped glass 'claw-beaker' probably from the Rhineland which was found in Castle Eden, County Durham (fig.19) - items which may have been family heirlooms by the time they were placed in the graves of their owners.

Such evidence indicates that accounts which describe the arrival of the Anglo-Saxons as a co-ordinated military invasion do not tell the whole story. It would appear that during the course of the fifth century increasing numbers of Germanic migrants came to live in the country in extended family groups with their own craftsmen, and in some cases they brought their treasured possessions with them.

Furthermore, it seems that although the Anglo-Saxons replaced the Britons as the dominant ethnic group, they did not entirely exterminate the native population. The Germanic dialects spoken by the Anglo-Saxons, which are ancestral to modern English, clearly replaced the Celtic languages of the Britons, and most of the places settled by them were given names in their own language, such as Ovingham, the village (ham) of Offa's people. But, beside such places,

fig.20 - Artist's impression of an Anglo-Saxon man and woman, based on archaeological evidence from Norton, Cleveland.

others, like Catterick and Carlisle (referring respectively, to places of war and fortification), and natural features in the landscape, such as the rivers Tyne, Wear and Don, retained their British names. Place-names such as these suggest that sufficient numbers of Britons continued to live in the area, ensuring the survival of words they used to refer to their surroundings. But perhaps the clearest indication that Britons continued to live in the region after the coming of the Anglo-Saxons is found in a number of place-names which contain the Old English word *walh*, meaning 'Britons': Walbrook and Walburn, in Yorkshire, were places where Britons lived by streams and Waldon was the valley of the Britons.

The cumulative effect of such evidence suggests that not only did the Anglo-Saxons migrate to and settle in England in family groups, but that the native British population also continued to live alongside the newcomers, and ultimately intermarried with them, in many parts of the country for some time. Certainly in the north where civilian society had always been comparatively under-developed there was apparently less disruption of the Romano-British population than may have occurred elsewhere in lowland Britain.

The Anglo-Saxons in the North

By the sixth century the people living in the north of Britain were predominantly Angles, Germanic peoples who migrated from the Netherlands and southern Scandinavia. Like most immigrant peoples, they maintained close contacts with their ancestral homelands for many generations. In the mid-sixth century, it has been suggested that one of their kings equipped his sister with an armed fleet so she could pursue her wayward fiancé, a prince of the continental Germans.

In their adopted homeland, the Angles tended to settle in the countryside, in the rural settlements inhabited by Britons and in new settlements of their own. As their economy was based largely on agriculture they had little need of the urban

fig.21 - Artist's impression of the early Anglian settlement at West Heslerton, North Yorkshire, based on archaeological evidence.

centres which had been so crucial to the economic and military organisation of the Roman Empire.

At West Heslerton (*fig.21*), in the Vale of Pickering, for instance, there was a large village occupied by Britons during the fourth and fifth centuries; by the end of the fifth century large numbers of Angles were also living there. Recent excavation of their cemetery shows that the Anglian men (who were farmers rather than warriors) were significantly taller than their British neighbours, and the women who lived with them wore brooches that are closely paralleled in southern Scandinavia, the northernmost homelands of the Angles.

Nine miles from the Roman fort at Malton, the village may have been the focus of a religious cult in the late Roman period. For the newly arrived Angles, it offered rich valley and hill soils, a navigable river with good supplies of fish and water, and ease of access to the sea, facilitating communication and trade with other settlements both in England and in continental Europe.

The village of West Heslerton itself was large, with over 150 houses, workshops and storage huts, all arranged into specific areas of activity: one for housing, one for craft and industry, and one for agricultural processing. The housing, separated from the industrial areas by the river, was further divided into separate 'neighbourhoods' so that those of higher social status lived together in one section. The houses themselves were all rectangular, built of upright timbers with thatched roofs, and heated by an open fire inside; some had small fenced enclosures adjacent to the houses. The agricultural lands of the village were used for mixed farming - for raising animals and growing grain. This produce, along with a regular supply of meat, fish and vegetables provided the inhabitants with a well-balanced diet. The industrial centre supplied most of the daily needs; tools were manufactured and cloth was woven. The villagers also had access to a wide range of imported objects: cowrie shells from the Red Sea or Indian Ocean, ivory from Africa, hone or sharpening stones from Scandinavia and quern stones from the Rhineland for grinding their grain.

Beasts and Serpents: The Art of the Early Anglo-Saxons

The jewellery and everyday items used by the Anglo-Saxons who lived in such communities from the fifth century onwards are, at first sight, insignificant objects when compared with the mass-produced artwork of the Romano-British. Nevertheless, almost everything the Anglo-Saxons used was decorated, from their

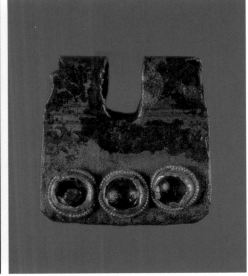

fig.22 - 6th-century bow brooches from Maltby, Cleveland, showing the variegated effects of Anglo-Saxon metalwork.
Cleveland Archaeology Section.

fig.23 - 7th-century gold sleeve-fastener with garnet inlay from Boldon, Tyne & Wear.
Museum of Antiquities, University of Newcastle upon Tyne.

ships to the hand-made pottery in which they stored their food. Patterns were carved on the prows of their ships; geometric designs were stamped onto the pots. Their clothes, made of linen and coarsely woven wool, were also decorated, with strips finely woven into geometric designs.

It is the jewellery that provides the clearest insight into their artistic traditions. Sleeve-clasps, buckles and brooches were decorated with a rich repertoire of zoomorphic (stylised animal) motifs that fill the surfaces and sometimes determine the shapes of the objects. One of the brooches from West Heslerton (*fig.24*), for example, a square-headed brooch with an ornate foot-plate, contains a whole menagerie of creatures in the decoration covering its surface, while further beasts form small protrusions on the outer edges. A round-eyed human face at the bottom of the foot-plate, stares up at the brooch. Set around its head is a thin strip of silver appliqué which forms a double-headed serpent: one head on either side of the human mask. These are confronted by two small animal profiles, consisting almost entirely of an eye with a large lid, protruding from the outer edge. More serpentine creatures fill the foot-plate. Their bodies are interlaced with each other and their stylised heads (composed of wide open jaws and prominent eyes) are placed symmetrically at the centre and on the upper corners. Additional, dog-like creatures, crouch on top of the square head-plate. On other brooches, such as a cruciform brooch from Benwell,

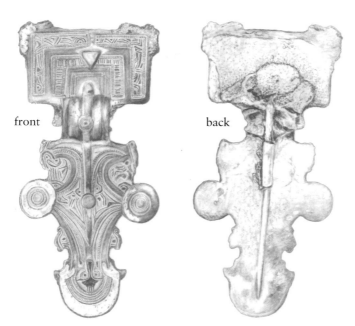

front   back

fig.24 - Square-headed brooch from West Heslerton, North Yorkshire, late 5th-early 6th century.

West Heslerton Parish Project.

fig.25 - Cruciform brooch from Benwell, Newcastle upon Tyne; 6th century.

Museum of Antiquities, University of Newcastle upon Tyne.

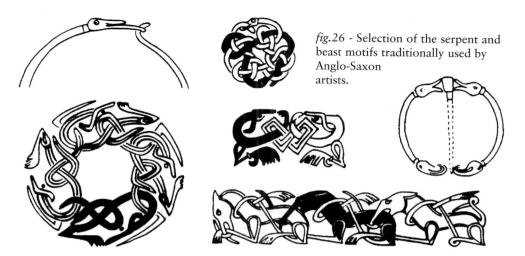

fig.26 - Selection of the serpent and beast motifs traditionally used by Anglo-Saxon artists.

a stylised horse's head (viewed from above) with exaggeratedly flared nostrils forms the foot-plate of the brooch (*fig.25*). In some cases such nostrils are so flared they evolve into yet more creatures: birds of prey with large curved beaks.

The art of the early Anglo-Saxons is characterised by repeated animal shapes and hidden forms. The animals, being so stylised, are not easy to decipher; the linear patterns used to describe their bodies and limbs serve to deliberately obscure them (*fig.26*). And such attention to pattern at the expense of form is further accentuated by the characteristic use of contrasting colours and different metalworking techniques. Different coloured metals were often used in the decoration of a single piece, as on the West Heslerton brooch and brooches from Norton. Gold, silver and gilt-bronze were used to offset each other, and the contrasts were highlighted with niello-work (dark coloured silver sulphate set in the grooves of the designs). The surface could be further varied with delicate filigree beading overlaid on the cast and beaten metals of the main field of decoration. The contrasts achieved with such methods were further emphasised by the use of inlaid semi-precious stones, such as garnet, and very occasionally amber (as on a 'brooch' from Ripon), fragments of white shell, and even pieces of coloured glass. There was also an apparent dislike of empty spaces on the Anglo-Saxon metalwork; plain surfaces are rare and usually occur only as focal points which contrast, and so emphasise, the richly ornamented panels around them (*figs.22-24*).

Together, these materials and techniques provided brilliantly shining, multi-faceted surfaces, but they also served to disguise the form of the stylised zoomorphic patterns which formed the basis of the decoration. Overall, the art of the early Anglo-Saxons was a non-representational art dominated by linear, geometric and symmetrical patterns, by contrasts, and the effect of light hitting variegated surfaces.

Legend

1. Milfield
2. Yeavering
3. Thirlings
4. Heavenfield
5. Warden
6. Corbridge
7. Hexham
8. Bywell
9. **NEWCASTLE UPON TYNE**
10. Pittington
11. South Church Auckland
12. Hart
13. Norton
14. Stanwick
15. Darlington
16. Sockburn
17. Kirkdale

Iona

Restenneth
Nechtanesmere

Firth of Tay

Dunadd

Firth of Forth

Dumbarton

Abercorn
Aberlady
Dunbar
Doon Hill
EDINBURGH
Traprain Law
Coldingham

Firth of Clyde

Norham
Lindisfarne
River Tweed

Old Melrose
Sprouston
Bamburgh
New Bewick

Jedburgh

Nith Bridge
Stidriggs
Closeburn

Ladyswell
Holystone
Rothbury
Nunny Kirk
Woodhorn

DUMFRIES
Hoddam
Bewcastle
Birtley
Bolam
Simonburn

Ruthwell
HADRIAN'S WALL
Tynemouth
River Tyn

Mote of Mark
Birdoswald
Jarrow
Monkwearmouth
River W

Kirkmadrine
CARLISLE
Chester le Street
Hurbuck
Seaham
Easington

Whithorn
Penrith
DURHAM
Hartlepool

Solway Firth
Dacre
Simy Folds
Escomb
Binchester
R

Morland
Billingham

STAINMOOR PASS
Gilling
Maltby
W

Gosforth
Easby
Croft on Tees
Lastingham

Irton
Catterick

Isle of Man
Heversham
Masham
Stonegrave
We

Ripon
Hovingham

Heysham
Green Hammerton

Ikley
YORK

Whalley
Otley
Sancton

Penwortham (?)
LEEDS
Ledsham

Dewsbury
Barton on Humber

Crofton
Hatfield Chase
Sc

River Mersey
MANCHESTER
DONCASTER

*fig.*27 -
Map of
Anglo-Saxon
Northumbria

IV

THE FORMATION OF A CHRISTIAN KINGDOM

The Ruling Families of Northumbria

The leaders of the early Anglian settlers of Northumbria are unknown, but by the mid-sixth century the region was dominated by two ruling dynasties. One controlled the land north of the River Tees, an area known by its British name, 'Bernicia' (the land of the mountain passes); the other held 'Deira' (sometimes identified as the land of the waters), to the south of the Tees. Both regions are assumed to have been native British territories, formed in the aftermath of the Roman occupation, and then taken over by the Anglo-Saxons.

fig.28 - Hanging bowl from Capheaton, Northumberland. Although this particular bowl is probably of Anglo-Saxon manufacture, bowls of this type were often acquired by the Anglo-Saxons from the British as loot in the early stages of their settlement in the British territories; 7th century.

Museum of Antiquities, University of Newcastle upon Tyne.

The original boundaries of Bernicia are unknown, but in 547 they were extended northwards by Ida, the leader of the Anglian royal family of Bernicia, to include a tract of land centred on Bamburgh. Apart from this little is known of Ida, but under his grandson, Æthelfrith, Bernicia came to dominate the North. He united Northumbria by conquering Deira and marrying Acha, the sister of the king. He also overpowered the British kingdoms of Strathclyde and Rheged (centred on Dumbarton and Carlisle), and in 603 he defeated the Scots of Dalriada (Argyll). At Chester, two years later, he took control of the British kingdom of Powys.

When Æthelfrith seized Deira its king, Edwin, was forced into exile. At first he sought protection in North Wales and the East Midlands (Mercia), where he married one of the royal princesses, Cwenburh. But when Æthelfrith turned his attentions in this direction Edwin took sanctuary with the king of the East Angles, Rædwald. Learning of this, and seeking to eliminate him as a focus of discontent, Æthelfrith sent ambassadors to Rædwald's court, requesting Edwin's extradition (or assassination). However, Rædwald's wife persuaded her husband to reject these overtures, and instead Rædwald and Edwin plotted to overthrow the Bernicians. In 616 they led an army against Æthelfrith, killed him in battle and forced his sons, Oswald and Oswiu, into exile in the far north: to the island of Iona.

Established as king of Northumbria, and having allies in East Anglia and Mercia, Edwin proceeded to extend his realm with further political unions and territorial conquests. One of his first alliances was made with Eadbald, the king of Kent. The coalition was sealed with Edwin's marriage to Æthelburh, Eadbald's sister; it is not known what happened to his first wife. Soon after this Edwin survived an assassination attempt orchestrated by the king of the West Saxons; his response was to take an army south into Wessex and rout it. He then moved into North Wales, defeated Cadwalla of Gwynedd, and took possession of Anglesey and the Isle of Man. Under the rule of Æthelfrith and then Edwin, Northumbria had become a kingdom of considerable size and power.

The Conversions of the North

When Edwin married Æthelburh, he married the daughter of the first Christian king of Anglo-Saxon England, Æthelbert of Kent, who had been converted to Christianity by missionaries from Rome in 597. According to Bede, however, the story of this conversion and that of Northumbria actually began some years earlier with the capture of some Anglian children from Deira who, being taken into

OSWALD (605-642)

As the son of Æthelfrith and his Deiran wife Acha, Oswald was forced to flee, at the age of 11, into exile with his brothers and sister (Æbbe) when their father was killed in battle against Rædwald and Edwin. For eighteen years he lived among the Scots of Dalriada, in mainland Scotland and northern Ireland. It was during this time that he was converted to Christianity and baptised on Iona. In 634 he returned to Northumbria to wrest the kingdom from Cadwalla of Gwynedd, who had defeated Edwin a year earlier.

For eight years Oswald ruled the kingdom, re-establishing Northumbrian dominance over Lindsey (modern-day Lincolnshire) and Mercia, and regaining control in southern England by forming an alliance with the West Saxons, Edwin's traditional enemies. This was a union which ensured there would be little retaliation from Kent. Indeed, it forced Edwin's widow Æthelburh to send their children away from Kent to Dagobert, the king of Franks, for protection, so great was her fear of Oswald's power. In 642, however, Oswald was killed at 'Maserfelth' (or Mæs Cogwy), traditionally identified as Old Oswestry, in battle against Penda of Mercia and the Britons of Powys. It is a measure of his reputation that he was remembered (as 'Oswald Brightsword') in the Welsh verse sagas.

Oswald's fame was not, however, due simply to his military and political standing. He also had a reputation as a devout Christian king responsible for firmly establishing Christianity in the north. He is reputed to have had a vision of St Columba on the eve of the battle of Heavenfield, and as soon as he was established as king he organised the foundation of a bishopric on Holy Island. As a Christian king he was credited with devoting much of his time to prayer and with acts of great generosity. Bede records how, on Easter Day, while feasting with Aidan and his thanes, Oswald gave to the poor gathered at his doors, his own food and a silver dish, which he ordered to be broken up and distributed amongst them.

At his death his head, arms and hands were severed and displayed on the field of battle by his enemies, but they were recovered by his brother and deposited, as relics, in the churches at Lindisfarne and Bamburgh; his body was eventually buried at Bardney (Lincolnshire). These sites were very quickly associated with miracles of healing and even of restoring the dead to life. Such events, as well as his actions in life, ensured his establishment as one of the first royal saints of Anglo-Saxon England.

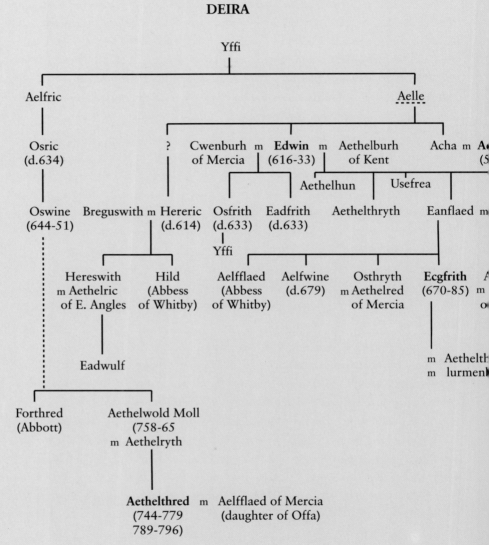

DEIRA

Yffi

Aelfric — Aelle

Osric (d.634) — ? — Cwenburh m Edwin m Aethelburh — Acha m Aᵉ
of Mercia (616-33) of Kent (5

Aethelhun — Usefrea

Oswine (644-51) — Breguswith m Hereric (d.614) — Osfrith (d.633) — Eadfrith (d.633) — Aethelthryth — Eanflaed m

Yffi

Hereswith m Aethelric of E. Angles — Hild (Abbess of Whitby) — Aelfflaed (Abbess of Whitby) — Aelfwine (d.679) — Osthryth m Aethelred of Mercia — Ecgfrith (670-85) m — A m o

Eadwulf

m Aethelth
m lurmenb

Forthred (Abbott) — Aethelwold Moll (758-65 m Aethelryth)

Aethelthred m Aelfflaed of Mercia
(744-779 (daughter of Offa)
789-796)

fig.29 - The ruling dynasties of Anglo-Saxon Northumbria

BERNICIA

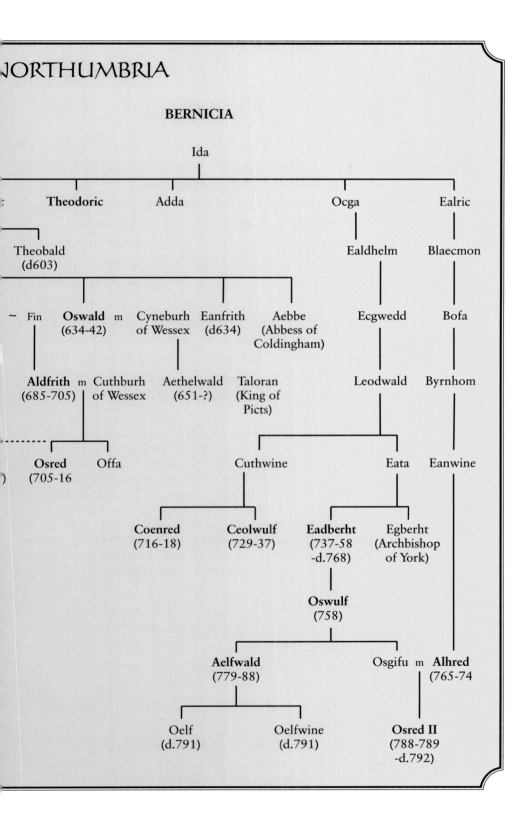

Ida

Theodoric   Adda   Ocga   Ealric

Theobald (d603)   Ealdhelm   Blaecmon

~   Fin   **Oswald** m (634-42)   Cyneburh of Wessex   Eanfrith (d634)   Aebbe (Abbess of Coldingham)   Ecgwedd   Bofa

Aldfrith m (685-705)   Cuthburh of Wessex   Aethelwald (651-?)   Taloran (King of Picts)   Leodwald   Byrnhom

)   **Osred** (705-16   Offa   Cuthwine   Eata   Eanwine

Coenred (716-18)   **Ceolwulf** (729-37)   **Eadberht** (737-58 -d.768)   Egberht (Archbishop of York)

Oswulf (758)

Aelfwald (779-88)   Osgifu m **Alhred** (765-74

Oelf (d.791)   Oelfwine (d.791)   **Osred II** (788-789 -d.792)

slavery, ended up in the slave-market of Rome. Seeing these "angelic" children, and learning that they came from a land which had not yet been introduced to Christianity, Pope Gregory, so the tale goes, sent a large mission headed by Augustine with instructions to convert the Anglo-Saxons and establish archbishoprics at Canterbury and York.

Thus, when Æthelburh came north as Edwin's queen, she came armed with a marriage contract granting her full religious freedom, a promise that her husband would consider conversion to Christianity, and a mission led by an Italian bishop, Paulinus. Edwin, however, was not easily persuaded that he should convert; given that there were no Christian kings in Anglo-Saxon England at this time (outside Kent), his reluctance is not too surprising. It seems, in fact, to have taken a whole series of events to finally convince him of the merits of Christianity: Æthelburh's safe delivery of a daughter, Eanflæd; a masterly insight by Paulinus into his innermost secrets; his escape from the assassin's dagger and subsequent victory over Wessex; and his domination of most of Anglo-Saxon England. But before he was finally baptised, Edwin still felt the need to discuss the issue with his advisers.

The council which he summoned took place at Goodmanham near York, the site of a major shrine of Deira, and after some initial debate, Edwin received the support of his counsellors for, as one of them pointed out:

> "When we compare the present life of man on earth with that time of which we have no knowledge, it seems to me like the swift flight of a sparrow through the room where you sit at dinner on a winter's day with your thanes and counsellors. In the midst there is a good fire to warm the hall; outside the storms of winter rain and snow are raging. This sparrow flies swiftly in through one door, and out through another. While he is within, he is safe from the winter storms; but after a brief moment of comfort, he vanishes from sight into the dark wintry world from which he had emerged. Even so man appears on earth for a while; but of what went before, or of what is to follow, we know nothing. If, therefore, this new doctrine contains something more certain, it seems only right that we should follow it."
>
> (Bede, *Ecclesiastical History* II, 13)

The response of the chief priest was equally positive, though somewhat more melodramatic. Apparently inspired by "this new doctrine", he denounced his gods and his priesthood before the council, took up arms and mounted a stallion (both of which were forbidden to priests), and, watched by a large crowd who "concluded he was distracted", he rode into the temple, destroyed the idols, and burnt the shrine to the ground.

Shortly afterwards, at Easter in the year 627, Edwin, "along with all the nobility of the nation, and a large number of the common sort", was baptised at York in a wooden church Edwin himself had commissioned, and Paulinus was

fig.30 -
Funerary
monument of
the northern
British
Church, from
Ardwall Isle,
Dumfries &
Galloway.

Dumfries Museum.

installed as the bishop of York. In the months that followed, Bede tells us that Paulinus spent most of his time performing baptisms the length and breadth of Northumbria, with one ceremony at Yeavering lasting a marathon thirty-six days; even some of Edwin's political allies were persuaded to convert.

Whatever the religious convictions of such men, the public endorsement of Christianity had certain political advantages. With Edwin's subjugation of most of Anglo-Saxon England he faced unprecedented administrative problems, with which the clerics of the Church were able to help him. Christianity was also a means of cementing political alliances. Edwin's conversion gave him connections, not simply with Kent, but with the ruling dynasty of Gaul and Rome itself; it made him part of an extended, European-wide system of alliances. Significantly, when Edwin was killed in battle in 633, at Hatfield Chase, it was in an uprising led by men who had not submitted to the Church of Rome under Edwin's guidance, men who were not directly included in this alliance system: his Mercian and Welsh 'allies'.

With Edwin dead, Bede describes the kingdom as falling into paganism. Paulinus fled south to Kent with the queen, the royal children, and the Northumbrian 'crown jewels' which included a large gold cross and chalice. Their flight, however, was probably inspired more by fear of political reprisals than pagan hostility. For one member of Paulinus' mission, James the Deacon, remained behind in a village near Catterick where he spent his time teaching and baptising the local population. He was still alive some thirty years later when he is known to have attended a Church Council at Whitby. And, although one of the kings who defeated Edwin was a pagan (Penda of Mercia), the other, who replaced him as ruler of Northumbria, was a Christian: Cadwalla of Gwynedd, a man who traced his descent to the Votadini tribe who centuries earlier had lived in Bernicia.

Bede's description of Northumbria as reverting to 'paganism' under these men, therefore, is not entirely accurate. It was inspired by the fact that Cadwalla's brand of Christianity was not that of Augustine and his missionaries. It was, rather, the Christianity which had survived in the north and west, beyond the frontiers of Roman Britain, since the fifth century, but which was unacceptable to the Church of sixth-century Rome. Caught in a fifth-century 'time-warp', its doctrines and rituals were considered to be a travesty of Christianity.

Despite this, much of the material culture of this Church has survived, while the fledgling Church of Edwin and Paulinus, which lasted for barely five years, has disappeared without trace; there is no sign of the church buildings set up by Edwin and Paulinus at centres such as York, Catterick and Doncaster. However, the literature, funerary monuments, and archaeological remains of the northern and western British Church have survived. Much of the early history of England preserved in Bede's work, for instance, is based on the writings of a British monk named Gildas, who wrote his own history, *The Ruin of Britain*, at the turn of the sixth century. At Whithorn, on the northern shores of the Solway, in the British kingdom of Rheged, are the remains of a stone church which was built in the fifth century and remained in use until the seventh century when it was rebuilt by the Northumbrians. At sites like this there are numerous stone monuments, dated from the fifth century onwards, which are incised with Christian symbols (such as the cross and the chi-rho), and with short epitaphs recording the names of the dead and their families (*fig.30*).

It was an offshoot of this British Church, taken to Ireland by Patrick during the fifth century, which succeeded in converting the Northumbrians - barely two years after the death of Edwin and the collapse of his Church. For, when Æthelfrith's sons escaped into exile on Iona they fled to an island monastery in the kingdom of Dalriada whose rulers had ancient ties with the Scots of northern Ireland. It was from there that a royal prince of Ulster (known to future generations as St Columba), was exiled in 563. Arriving in Dalriada, he was granted land on Iona where he established a monastery (*fig.31*).

fig.31 - The monastic site on Iona.

It was there, far from Edwin, his allies and the Church of Rome, that Oswald and his brother were baptised in the seventh century. When news reached them that Edwin was dead and Cadwalla was ruling in his stead, Oswald raised a small army (with the support of the Dalriadans) and returned to Northumbria. Late in 634 he met and defeated Cadwalla at Heavenfield, near Hexham - after erecting a wooden cross and leading his army in prayer.

These were actions symbolic of the reign which was to follow, for almost immediately Oswald petitioned the abbot of Iona for missionaries to help him establish a Christian kingdom in Northumbria. An Irish monk, named Aidan, was sent and given land at Lindisfarne on Holy Island, within sight of the royal centre at Bamburgh (*fig.36*).

AIDAN (d.651)

Known as the 'Apostle of Northumbria', Aidan was the second missionary sent from Iona in response to Oswald's request for a bishop. The first had returned complaining of the recalcitrance of the Anglo-Saxons; he had been unable to teach them anything because, in his opinion, they were an obstinate and uncivilised people of barbarous temperament.

On his arrival in Northumbria in 635 Aidan established a bishopric at Lindisfarne close to the chief royal residence of Bamburgh on the land granted by Oswald, and during the next sixteen years oversaw the establishment of the Church in Northumbria through the foundation of a series of monasteries on land donated by members of the Northumbrian aristocracy. In many cases he selected the (royal) abbots and abbesses personally. In this work Aidan never lost the support of the rulers of Northumbria. He involved them in his mission, even to the extent of using Oswald as his interpreter when addressing the members of the Anglo-Saxon court. He was often in attendance at the royal courts, particularly when the king was in residence at Bamburgh: he was present at Oswald's feast on Easter Day when the food and silver plate from the royal table were distributed to the poor; and he was outside the church in Bamburgh when he died.

Aidan was not simply a statesman overseeing the establishment of the Church in Northumbria, however. He lived a life of obvious poverty and charity, using gifts of money, not for personal benefit or even to enrich his foundations, but to help the poor and ransom slaves from captivity. He spent much of his time travelling (on foot) round the Northumbrian countryside preaching and baptising the population. He was outspoken in his attacks on wrongdoers, regardless of their rank; even his close friend, Oswine, the sub-king of Deira, was not excluded from his condemnation.

At his death he was buried in the church at Lindisfarne, to the right of the high altar. During his life he was credited with performing numerous miracles, and in death he became the focus of a number of healing miracles. Indeed, chips of wood from the support against which he was leaning when he died were reputed to have curative powers and the post itself survived more than one fire, being re-used in the building of three successive churches. When Colman left Northumbria after the Synod of Whitby in 664 he took some of Aidan's remains with him to Iona.

fig.32 - The 7th-century portable altar of St Cuthbert, which was given a silver casing in the 8th century. *Durham Cathedral Treasury.*

The Church of Aidan and his companions was very different to that which had been brought to Kent by Augustine. That was a centrally organised Church divided into administrative units (dioceses) with a hierarchy of clergy headed by archbishops and bishops. In the centuries during which Rome had been cut off from the British Isles, however, the Irish Church had not retained this structure. Instead, the diocesan system was integrated into a monastic organisation which evolved in keeping with the tribal structures of secular Irish society. This primarily monastic Church was composed of groups of men and women living in small, often remote, communities who devoted their lives to a daily ritual of prayer and worship. They produced their own food and clothing, and above all, the books, vestments and vessels needed for their acts of worship. Each community was ruled by an abbot, or, if it was a convent or double-monastery (inhabited by both monks and nuns), by an abbess.

fig.33 - Portable chalice from Hexham, Northumberland, of the type which would have been carried by a priest holding services in areas where no churches had yet been established. *Hexham Abbey.*

fig.34 - Modern statue of St. Aidan, Lindisfarne.

fig.35 - The medieval ruins of Lindisfarne Priory
on the site of Aidan's monastery

The Early Church of Northumbria

This was the ecclesiastical organisation brought to Northumbria by Aidan and which spread throughout the North, with 'daughter-houses', dependent on the 'mother-house' at Lindisfarne, being founded at Coldingham, Hartlepool, Lastingham, Whitby (*fig.37*), and Hackness. These were sites strategically placed near old, established route ways, by navigable rivers, or on prominent headlands which gave commanding views of the sea or surrounding countryside and easy access to communication and trade routes.

The land was granted by members of the royal family as working estates along with the farm-labourers living on them; when the land around Ripon, in North Yorkshire, was given to the Church some forty families were involved in the transfer. The founding abbots and abbesses to whom these estates were given, were members of the royal family itself. Æbbe, the abbess of Coldingham, was the sister of Oswald and Oswiu, and Edwin's cousin, Hild, was the abbess, first of Hartlepool and then of Whitby, where she was followed by Ælfflæd, daughter, grand-daughter, sister and niece of successive kings of Northumbria.

Under the rule of men and women so closely related to the secular rulers of the kingdom, the early Church of Northumbria was an integral part of its political, social and economic structures. But it was also a religious institution; its monastic communities were dedicated to the daily ritual of prayer and many of the inhabitants were involved in missionary activity. Aidan made frequent excursions "to preach in the country round about" (Bede, *Ecclesiastical History* III, 5). On such trips the monks would carry with them a staff and a satchel containing all they needed to perform their services: a bell, portable altar (*fig.32*), a chalice (*fig.33*) and service-books.

The early monastic centres themselves were complex settlements built of wood and thatch with enclosing banks and ditches (often circular) defining their outer boundaries. The church, the focus of the community, was set at its centre; the cemetery would be laid out close by. The living quarters of the monks and nuns were often no more than small single-roomed structures where they spent their days in prayer and work: weaving, embroidering cloths for the church, reading or copying manuscripts. Separated from these structures were other buildings, including the school, hospital and accommodation for guests, stores and workshops.

fig.36 - Aerial view of Bamburgh Castle, site of an Anglo-Saxon royal palace overlooking the monastery of Lindisfarne on Holy Island (visible in the far distance).

fig.37 - Whitby, medieval ruins on the site of the double monastery founded by St Hild in the 7th century.

HILD (614-680)

Hild was a princess of the Deiran dynasty, and, although a nun for nearly half her life, exercised considerable influence in affairs of state as abbess of the royal monastic foundation at Whitby.

Born while her parents were in exile during Æthelfrith's reign, her early life followed the fortunes of her great-uncle Edwin. She probably spent her infancy in East Anglia, moving to Northumbria after 616. At the age of 13 she was baptised by Paulinus. With Edwin's death in 632 she may have returned to East Anglia where her sister was queen, and where the Gallic Church (an offshoot of the Irish Church) was influential. Whether this was the case, or whether she remained in Northumbria to encounter the Irish Church introduced there by Oswald and Aidan, she was converted to its traditions and decided to enter the double monastery at Chelles (near Paris). On the eve of her departure, however, she was recalled to Northumbria by Aidan and persuaded to remain there, initially to found a new monastery on the north banks of the Wear. Subsequently she became abbess, first of Hartlepool, and then of Whitby, a double monastery founded by Oswiu after his victory over Penda in 655.

Whitby remained very much a royal centre under Hild and her immediate successors: Eanflæd (Oswiu's widow) and Ælfflæd, their daughter, dedicated to God by Oswiu in return for his victory at Winwæd. It was the burial place of the Deiran royal family; both Edwin and Oswiu were interred there. And, it was at Whitby that Oswiu held the Synod that was to determine the nature of the Northumbrian Church in 664. Although she accepted the outcome of this council, Hild seems to have been opposed to Wilfrid as a result of his part in the proceedings; she played an influential role in his fall, in 678, from the power (both secular and ecclesiastical) which he had gained throughout Northumbria.

Apart from being so deeply involved in affairs of state, Hild also seems to have encouraged a certain amount of learning and scholarship at Whitby. One of the first saint's lives to be written in England was composed there, a life of St Gregory which demonstrates detailed knowledge of the Roman pope. And it was at Whitby that Cædmon was first inspired to compose Christian poems in the manner of an English scop, an achievement encouraged by Hild. Her monastery was also the home of no fewer than five Anglo-Saxon bishops, one of whom supplanted Wilfrid at York in 678.

She died in 680, the year that the seven-year old Bede entered the monastery of Wearmouth and began his education, which was to enable him to write, in his Ecclesiastical History, the only life of Hild known to us.

The Church and its Art

The artefacts made by the scribes and craftsmen working in these monasteries for religious use were, regardless of the medium (metalwork, textile, stone or parchment), decorated with motifs derived from both the art of the Irish Church and that traditionally used in the non-Christian art of the Anglo-Saxons.

fig.38 - The 7th-century gold and garnet pendant cross of St Cuthbert. *Durham Cathedral Treasury.*

Gold pendant crosses, such as the one worn by St Cuthbert, were made of gold filigree work and inlaid with small pieces of garnet and shell, typical of seventh-century Anglo-Saxon metalwork (*fig.38*). Styli, used to write on wax tablets, and gilt-metal mounts made to embellish and reinforce the covers of books, were decorated with the zoomorphic and geometric interlacing patterns, long-familiar in Germanic, Anglo-Saxon art. Some artefacts, such as the mounts from Whitby, continue the tradition of containing hidden shapes within their decoration. The mounts are composed of two crosses with rounded terminals which have been super-imposed on each other, but the varied interlace patterns used to fill the spaces within the arms and terminals of the crosses serve to disguise the basic design.

The books bound with such mounts were themselves new to Anglo-Saxon society, and so they were written in the scripts used by the Irish scribes. One of these was a very distinctive rounded script, produced with great labour and care, known as 'insular half uncial'; the other was a more fluid, less formal, pointed script known as 'insular minuscule'. Developed in Ireland between the fourth and sixth centuries these scripts, once introduced to Anglo-Saxon Northumbria, were

fig.39 - Funerary 'pillow-stone' from Lindisfarne, Northumberland, inscribed (in runes and Anglo-Saxon capitals) with the name OSGYÐ; mid-7th to mid-8th century.
Lindisfarne Priory Museum.

reproduced in the northern monastic centres, not only in manuscripts (handwritten books) but also in other media, such as carved stone monuments. The more formal script was incised on small funerary stones (the so-called 'pillow stones' found at monasteries such as Lindisfarne (*fig.39*), Hartlepool and Whitby) to record the names of the dead monks and nuns. On such monuments it was sometimes accompanied by a runic script, long used by the Germanic Anglo-Saxons to inscribe names and short epithets onto pottery, weapons and jewellery.

But, it was in the manuscripts that the Irish-derived scripts were reproduced most frequently. The half uncial script was used to write a number of deluxe gospel books in the seventh century, and in one preserved at Durham it was used along with the finer, more pointed minuscule script (*fig.40*). This script, being less formal and easier to write than the half uncial, was more commonly used for non-biblical texts (such as histories and commentaries), and continued to be produced throughout the Anglo-Saxon period, long after the more laborious half uncial had ceased to be used. In the tenth century it was employed to write an English translation of the Latin text of the late seventh-century Lindisfarne Gospels which had been written in half uncial (*fig.74*).

In the northern centres where these Irish-derived scripts were employed, specific types of decorated pages and ornamental motifs were also produced. Some of these may have been developed by Irish scribes and artists in order to embellish their books during the first half of the seventh century. In the northern centres, however, such motifs were incorporated with others drawn from the (non-Christian) artistic repertoire of the Anglo-Saxons.

fig.40 - Text of the Lord's Prayer from a Gospel fragment (Durham Cathedral Library, MS A.II.10, f.3b), showing the insular half-uncial and minuscule scripts, and the mixed use of Anglo-Saxon interlacing and Celtic curvilinear motifs; mid-7th century.

Durham Cathedral Library.

fig.41 - Carpet page from the Book of Durrow, MS A.4.5 (57), f.3v, filled with abstract patterns; mid-7th century.

Trinity College Library, Dublin.

The Book of Durrow, produced in the first half of the seventh century, contains a number of 'carpet pages' (pages devoted entirely to abstract ornament), which have the effect of separating one part of the gospel text from another (*fig.41*). The decoration of some of these pages is composed of the curvilinear patterns of the Celtic Irish artistic repertoire: whorl, pelta, spiral and trumpet motifs (*fig.43*). But there are also carpet pages filled with the interlace patterns and intertwining beasts and serpents of Anglo-Saxon art.

The Irish system of using minute red dots to highlight significant passages in the biblical text was also used in these northern centres, as were the initial letters enlarged and decorated with curvilinear motifs which Irish scribes were using to mark the beginning of important passages in the text. Again, these features were incorporated with the zoomorphic and interlace motifs of the Northumbrian Anglo-Saxon artists. In the Durham gospel fragment three enlarged letters fill one half of the page. They are decorated with varying interlace patterns very reminiscent of the gold and niello-work of Anglo-Saxon metalwork, and in each corner is a brightly coloured motif formed from finely executed spirals and peltas (*fig.40*).

Other illustrations indicate that the Irish and Anglo-Saxon decorative motifs were not the only ones which influenced the artists of these early seventh-century monastic centres; the art of the Pictish north was also used. The symbol of the calf

fig.42 - Bull featured on a Pictish 'symbol stone' from Burghead, Grampian; 7th century.

in the Book of Durrow has small spirals marking its joints; this is a technique not found in Anglo-Saxon animal art, nor in Irish art, but it is common on the carved symbol stones set up by the Picts in Scotland (*fig.42*).

The decoration of the early, seventh-century, manuscripts displays the early stages of an art which incorporated the designs and ornamental motifs of very distinct artistic traditions which, during the later seventh and eighth centuries, would produce a style identifiably different to the cultures which had originally inspired it: the 'insular' art of the Golden Age.

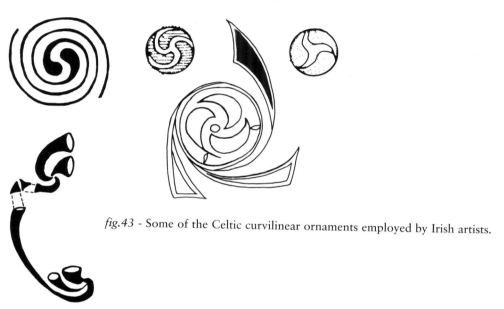

fig.43 - Some of the Celtic curvilinear ornaments employed by Irish artists.

V

THE GOLDEN AGE

Northumbrian Overlords

The establishment of Northumbria as a Christian kingdom coincided with the period when its rulers controlled most of Anglo-Saxon England. In his *Ecclesiastical History*, Bede lists seven such men. Three of these were the kings of Northumbria: Edwin, Oswald, and Oswiu. Their military and political power was a continuing force throughout the seventh century even though they were threatened by revolts and conspiracies.

Edwin was killed in an uprising led by the kings of Mercia and Gwynedd, men who owed him tribute. Oswald, too, was killed in battle, in 642, by Penda of Mercia who had been one of the leaders of the revolt against Edwin; this time he found an ally in Oswald's brother, Oswiu (three of whose children had been married into the Mercian royal family). On Oswald's death Oswiu took control of Bernicia, while his distant cousin Oswine, whose father had helped Penda defeat Edwin, was set up as king of Deira until he was assassinated by Oswiu in 651. Replacing Oswine with his son, Alhfrith, Oswiu then ruled Northumbria for nineteen years, surviving further attacks by the Mercians, whom he finally defeated in 655 at 'Winwæd', a place variously identified with Wentworth or the River Went, a tributary of the Don.

Despite such upheavals Northumbria remained a large and powerful realm. Oswald and Oswiu continued to control southern Pictland, Dalriada, Strathclyde, Rheged and East Anglia. Oswiu also maintained contact with Mercia through the marriages of his children, and with Kent, through his own marriage to Eanflæd, the daughter of Æthelburh (and Edwin). Their son Ecgfrith wielded much the same power as his father and uncle had done until he too was killed in battle, at

fig.44 - Artist's impression, based on archaeological evidence, of the royal Anglo-Saxon centre at Yeavering, Northumberland, as it might have been in the early 7th century.

Nechtansmere (Dunnichen in Tayside) in 685. It was only at this point, at the end of the seventh century, that the Britons of Strathclyde, the Dalriadan Scots and the Picts regained their lands and independence; the Northumbrian episcopal centre of the region, established at Abercorn, was abandoned.

Aldfrith (the illegitimate son of Oswiu and a princess of Ulster), who had sought "voluntary exile to gratify his love of wisdom" among the Irish on Iona during Ecgfrith's reign, succeeded his half-brother (Bede's *Prose Life of St Cuthbert* ch.24). Under him and his heirs, the kingdom of Northumbria remained a rich and secure realm within wide-ranging borders (the Solway and the Forth to the north, and the Humber and the Mersey in the south), until the second half of the eighth century.

Feasting and Singing in the Hall

Looking back on this period of Northumbrian supremacy, Bede was to regard it as an almost legendary golden age of peace and prosperity. Under Edwin, it was said, a woman could carry her child from one side of the country to the other without harm; brass bowls hung next to springs of water by the roadside for the use of travellers were not stolen or misused. The king himself would travel through his kingdom in stately processions headed by a royal banner (*Ecclesiastical History* II, 16). Despite their constant military campaigns, the Northumbrian kings clearly maintained a general sense of well-being, and in the royal centres from which they ruled, they lived lives of some ceremony and ritual.

Bamburgh and York were two of these centres. Others have been identified near Dewsbury and Leeds in West Yorkshire, at Edinburgh (Castle Rock) and Doon Hill (Lothian), and at Milfield and Yeavering in the foot-hills of the Cheviots. All were sites of British royal power which were appropriated by the leaders of the Anglo-Saxons when they took over Bernicia and Deira during the sixth century.

Excavations at Yeavering show that this particular royal centre, set on a plateau above the River Glen, was originally dominated by a British pagan temple. When the Anglo-Saxons took over the site they built, between this temple and a large corral set further down the slopes of the hill, a series of large wooden halls and a 'grandstand' (rather like a segment of a Roman-style amphitheatre) which at one time seated up to 320 people (*fig.44*).

The halls were extremely impressive buildings. One, built during Edwin's reign, was nearly 25m (82ft) long and 11m (36ft) wide. Its walls, built of large planks and plastered inside (in imitation of Roman buildings still visible in the landscape), rose to a height of at least 5m (16ft). With an entrance porch at one end and doors in each side wall, it was a great aisled structure consisting almost entirely of a long central hall with wooden pillars running down each side. Buildings such as this were not permanent residences. They were only used by the king when he visited the centre to collect the food-rents owed by his vassals in the region. The corral was probably used to keep the livestock, brought in on the hoof. While providing the ruler with his tribute, these visits also gave the people regular access to their king, enabling him to sit in judgement and settle local disputes. At Yeavering such gatherings may have taken place in the 'grandstand'.

As well as providing temporary housing for the king, the royal halls also functioned as places where, during a feast, he could regulate the law, entertain his warriors and reward their loyalty. On such occasions, the king sat on a raised throne at one end of the hall surrounded by his most trusted 'thanes' while his other followers sat at-tables filling the rest of the room. It was at one such feast that the attempt was made on Edwin's life. It was only the fact that he was surrounded by his thanes that saved him, for it was one of them who foiled the attack by throwing himself between the king and the assassin's blade.

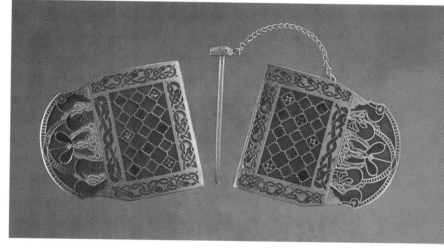

fig.45 - Shoulder-clasps from the early 7th-century ship burial at Sutton Hoo, Suffolk. Items such as these indicate the high-quality craftsmanship and value of the artefacts involved in the royal gift-giving ceremonies.
British Museum.

This was the ultimate expression of a warrior's loyalty; usually rewards were given for more general faithfulness of service to the king (and queen). The poetry of the Anglo-Saxons is filled with highly coloured descriptions of such ceremonies and the richness of the rewards distributed (*fig.45*). In the Old English poem 'Beowulf' the hero receives gifts from the king of the Danes for ridding them (and their royal hall) of the monster Grendel: a gold embroidered banner, an ornate sword, a crested helmet, a mail corslet, eight horses with gold plated bridles and one with a jewelled saddle, and ancient heirlooms for his followers; from the queen he received a gold neck-ring and corslet.

The point of such generosity was not simply to reward the warrior's heroism. It was also intended to demonstrate the honour and magnanimity of the king and queen, and although the poetic accounts are exaggerated in keeping with their heroic subject-matter, they nevertheless provide an insight into a ritual which formed an integral part of royal life. For it was through the regular payment of such gifts that the kings both rewarded and ensured the loyalty of their warriors; a king of the East Angles who failed to reward his followers adequately was forcibly removed from the throne. Sometimes land was given, but the most usual gifts were precious objects of gold and silver: jewelled swords and other military accoutrements, belts with golden buckles, precious arm-bands and necklaces, items taken as plunder from the battle-field.

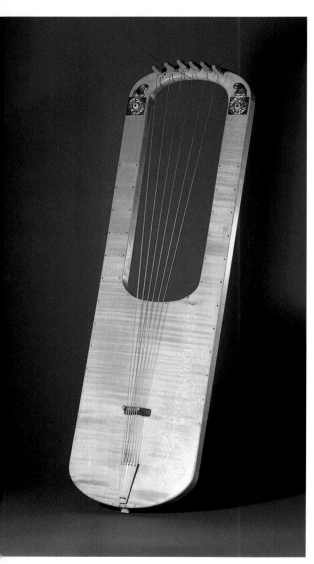

fig.46 - Reconstruction of the harp-like instrument found at Sutton Hoo. Such instruments would have been used by the scops (poets) for their recitals in the royal halls of the Anglo-Saxon kings.

British Museum.

The feasts at which such ceremonial gift-giving took place were also marked by performances of poetry: recitals given by poets, known as 'scops', who would chant their poems to the sound of harp music (*fig.46*). Composed while they were being performed from a store of memorised rhythmic phrases, the poems, which could be very lengthy, dealt with many subjects, from laments and elegies to accounts of the deeds of long-dead heroes. But it was the heroic epics which formed the most apt entertainment for the royal feasts, for such poems were the means by which the history of the kings and their people were preserved. Such stories celebrated the exploits of the king's ancestors, their successes in war and their mythical descent from the gods.

CUTHBERT (c.630-687)

The most famous of the Anglo-Saxon saints, Cuthbert was born into a noble Northumbrian family and, as was the practice among the Anglo-Saxon aristocracy, was placed with a foster mother at the age of eight and eventually entered military service. In 651, inspired by a vision of the soul of Aidan being carried to heaven at the moment of his death, Cuthbert left secular life and entered the monastery at Melrose, founded by one of Aidan's pupils, Eata. With Eata he went to Ripon which had been donated by Alhfrith, but rather than adopt the Roman practices advocated by Alhfrith, they soon returned to Melrose and Ripon was given to Wilfrid. On his return, and having survived an outbreak of plague, Cuthbert was made prior of Melrose.

He spent much of his time preaching in the surrounding countryside, often being away for a month at a time. On one occasion he went to preach among the Picts. His qualities as a teacher, his tact and ability to get on with people, which had earned him the post of guest-master at Ripon, also led Æbbe, the abbess of Coldingham, to seek his help in reforming her double-monastery when the nuns and monks had almost completely abandoned the religious life.

In 664, after the Synod of Whitby, Cuthbert was made prior of Lindisfarne, but in 676 he left the monastery for a life of seclusion on Inner Farne. Here, in the fashion of the Irish monastic hermitages, he built a circular wall of stones and turf to enclose an oratory, some small huts, and a garden. The life he led was one of isolation, hardship and asceticism, one advocated by the Irish monastic tradition as a means of martyrdom. His reputation, however, meant that visitors were common, and his counsel was regularly sought by other ecclesiastics and even the king and queen. As the king's adviser he warned Ecgfrith not to invade Ireland (advice which on this occasion was not heeded); after Ecgfrith's death at Nechtansmere, Cuthbert left Inner Farne to meet Ælfflæd on Coquet Island to discuss the return of Aldfrith.

While on Farne he had been elected bishop of Hexham in 685. Although he had left Ripon rather than abandon Irish ecclesiastical practices, Cuthbert had accepted the outcome of the Synod of Whitby, and acknowledged the authority of Rome and the need for order and unity in the Church. He served as bishop for less than two years until shortly before his death in 687.

Stories of his miracles, which involved not only cures but also prophecies and angelic visitations, began to grow, and his body, originally set in a stone-lined grave by the altar of the church at Lindisfarne, became a focus of pilgrimage after 698. Three versions of his life were written: one by an unknown monk of the Lindisfarne community and two by Bede, one in prose and one in verse.

WILFRID (634-709)

Wilfrid, one of the most influential figures in the formation of the Church in Northumbria, was a member of the Northumbrian aristocracy. At 14 he decided to pursue the religious life, and studied in the monastic school on Holy Island until, in 652 he left for the first of many trips to Rome. His companion on this journey was Benedict Biscop; theirs is the first known visit to Rome by the English. In Rome Wilfrid received instruction in matters of Roman orthodoxy before returning to England by way of Lyons where he took his monastic vows. On his arrival in Northumbria he was granted a number of landed estates by Alhfrith, who also introduced him to Agilbert, the Frankish bishop who ordained him priest. It was as the protegé of these men that Wilfrid was elected spokesman of the Romani at Whitby and then appointed bishop of Lindisfarne after Colman's departure for Ireland. To ensure the validity of his election Wilfrid travelled to Gaul to be ordained, but on his return he discovered that another monk, Chad, had been installed in his place.

Thereafter, Wilfrid's career was extremely turbulent. His involvement in the personal lives of the royal family of Northumbria and his extraordinary accumulation of land and wealth contributed to the fact that he was deprived of his episcopacy a total of three times (664-9, 678-86 and 691-706). It was Oswiu, for instance, who replaced Wilfrid with Chad after the Synod of Whitby. Then Iurminburgh, Ecgfrith's second wife, jealous of Wilfrid's influence, encouraged her husband's resentment of Wilfrid's role in the break-up of his first marriage. Thus, on the two occasions when Wilfrid appealed to Rome in person, successfully, to be reinstated as bishop, the papal verdict was ignored in Northumbria. Indeed, when he returned with his first papal decree in 680, Oswiu confined him to prison for nine months. When he was finally reinstated in 706 the extent of his diocese had been reduced to an area dependent on his monastery at Hexham; in 669 it had included the whole of Northumbria.

Despite such a troubled career Wilfrid's achievements were impressive. His unswerving enthusiasm for the Churches of Gaul and Rome inspired him to undertake impressive building projects at his own monastic foundations of Ripon and Hexham, and at the episcopal seat of York. He brought in artisans to help construct and decorate his buildings, and singers trained in the Roman chant to instruct others in the order of the liturgy. And, he ran his monasteries according to the Rule of St Benedict which he is credited with introducing to Northumbria. While out of office Wilfrid was also an active missionary. He was the first Anglo-Saxon to preach overseas, in Frisia, and he was instrumental in converting the South Saxons, nearly the last pagan nation of Anglo-Saxon England.

The Church Triumphant

It was under the rule of such kings that Northumbrian culture achieved its maximum expression in the so-called 'Golden Age' of the late seventh and eighth centuries. But this flowering of the arts was not due entirely to the political well-being of the kingdom, for the military campaigns which formed the basis of Northumbrian royal power were also a source of insecurity, and throughout the eighth century Bernicians and Deirans, fathers and sons, brothers and distant cousins replaced each other as rulers with ever-increasing frequency.

Against this unsettled background, it was the Church which formed the real centre of power, providing the stability and prosperity the secular rulers could not. It was Ælfflæd, the royal abbess of Whitby (with the consent of Cuthbert, the abbot and bishop of Lindisfarne), who invited her half-brother Aldfrith out of exile to rule Northumbria in 685. And rulers in the eighth-century depended as much on the approval of the archbishops of York (who were members of the Bernician royal family), as on the backing of their followers for any political and military successes they enjoyed. Such impressive ecclesiastical power was not due entirely to the family ties of the Northumbrian prelates, however. It owed something to the fact that in the second half of the seventh century the Church in Northumbria was re-united with that of Rome and the European mainland.

When Oswiu's son Alhfrith became sub-king of Deira he was introduced to the Roman Church by a Northumbrian nobleman, named Wilfrid, who had travelled to Rome and Gaul after receiving his initial schooling in the monastery at Lindisfarne. In the course of his travels Wilfrid became fully aware of the differences between the Roman and Irish Churches. Of the two, the Irish Church was deemed to be dangerously heretical; its digressions were many, and covered all aspects of church life, from minor fashions of dress to major points of doctrine.

The tonsure of an Irish monk, for example, was not like that of a Roman monk who shaved the crown of his head, leaving a ring of hair in imitation of the crown of thorns worn by Christ at the crucifixion; the Irish seem to have merely shaved the front of their heads, from ear to ear, producing a receding hairline. But, it was the absence of an established ecclesiastical hierarchy of bishops and archbishops, and the Irish method of calculating when Easter should be celebrated which were the main points of contention. This last was not simply a matter of doctrine. In the royal household of Northumbria it meant that Oswiu, following the Irish calendar of Church feasts, celebrated Easter a week before his wife Eanflæd who, having been raised in Kent, followed the Roman calendar. The result was, that while Eanflæd kept the fast of Lent, Oswiu was feasting, celebrating the Resurrection of Christ.

Thus, under pressure from all sides Oswiu agreed to hold a Synod (Church Council) at Whitby in 664 to determine which tradition should be followed. The cause of the Irish Church, supported by Oswiu and Hild, was argued by Colman, the abbot of Lindisfarne. Against his father, and supporting the cause of the Church of Rome, was Alhfrith who was accompanied by Agilberht (a bishop from Gaul and a friend of Wilfrid) and James the Deacon (the surviving member of Paulinus' Roman mission to Northumbria thirty years earlier). They selected Wilfrid to argue their case. In the end Oswiu decided in favour of Rome, for as Wilfrid pointed out, Peter, the patron saint of the Church at Rome, held the keys to heaven; St John, the patron saint of the Irish Church, did not. His decision meant that, after 664, the Church in Northumbria was united under the banner of Roman orthodoxy. Those, like Colman, who would not conform left Northumbria for Iona and northern Ireland.

It was from this time onwards that the Northumbrian Church began to grow in status and prestige. Its wealth, derived from its landed estates, its monopolies in valuable commodities, such as lead, and its virtual control of shipping (and, therefore, trade), meant many monasteries functioned as 'ecclesiastical courts'. Indeed, in their general appearance aristocratic churchmen and women could rival members of the royal household. Wilfrid cultivated a splendid episcopal image, riding a fine horse, wearing clothes that marked him as the equal of the king and keeping an enormous retinue of followers. When attacked by pagan Anglo-Saxons on the shores of Sussex he was accompanied by 120 armed men who, like faithful warriors, vowed "that they would either find death with honour or life with victory" (*Life of Wilfrid* ch.13). For Wilfrid, however, this life-style was regarded as a ploy, necessary in his negotiations with the kings and queens of Northumbria. Beneath his finery he wore the hair-shirt of an ascetic. He was an active patron of hermits and an enthusiastic advocate of the religious life for women. He encouraged Ecgfrith's wife in her virginity through twelve years of marriage (a course of action which did not endear him to the king). He was also an active missionary: in Sussex and Frisia.

But although Wilfrid may have regarded an outwardly extravagant life-style as a justifiable means to an end, others were less circumspect and spent their lives in "laughter, jests, tales, feasting and drunkenness" and acquiring gold and silver (Bede's *Letter to Ecgbert of York*). Even Aidan's foundation at Lindisfarne enjoyed 'secular' activities. Like the kings and their followers, the monks listened to the songs of the scops celebrating the deeds of the legendary heroes of old while they feasted.

fig.47 - The man symbol of the Evangelist Matthew, from the Book of Durrow, f.21v; the hair-line resembles that of the Irish tonsure; mid-7th century.
Trinity College Library, Dublin.

RIPON AND HEXHAM

Ripon and Hexham are the Anglo-Saxon monasteries most closely associated with Wilfrid. He was installed as abbot of Ripon by Alhfrith in 660, after the monks of Melrose had departed, refusing to conform to the Roman practices advocated by their patron. Hexham was donated by Ecgfrith's first queen, Æthelthryth, in about 672.

The church at Ripon, begun shortly after Wilfrid was consecrated bishop in 665, was built of stone by masons and artisans brought over from Gaul, and like the churches there and in Italy it was a basilican church with columns and side aisles. Its importance was established at the dedication ceremony, held in 672, which was attended by most of the dignitaries of Northumbria, including the king. For the occasion Wilfrid had acquired a gospel book written in gold on purple parchment in the manner of imperial Roman manuscripts. The altar was covered in purple cloth woven with gold, and during the service Wilfrid read a list of the lands which had been donated to the monastery. The ceremony was followed by three days of feasting.

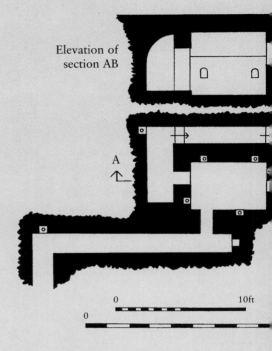

Elevation of section AB

A

0   10ft

0

fig.48 - Plan and elevation of the crypt built by Wilfrid under his church at Ripon.
After Taylor and Taylor 1978.

In the same year building work began on the church at Hexham. Completed in 678, it too was a large, basilican-style church, described by Wilfrid's biographer Eddius Stephanus, as being very long and high, with columns, side aisles, numerous passages, and spiral staircases. His comparison of the church with those in Italy was repeated some five centuries later, by William of Malmesbury, who asserted that it was still possible, in the twelfth century, to see at Hexham all the glories of Rome.

Wilfrid also built at least two (possibly three), other churches at Hexham. Two have been identified from archaeological remains as having stood to the south-east and north-west of Wilfrid's main basilica, and excavations have also revealed the presence of a small chapel to the east of this church. A multiplicity of churches at a single site was not unusual in Anglo-Saxon England. It occurs elsewhere in Northumbria at Jarrow and Wearmouth, and at Bywell and Carlisle. It was a practice introduced from Gaul where it occurs at monastic centres such as Nivelles (in Belgium) and Corbie (in northern France).

Unfortunately, nothing remains of Wilfrid's stone churches that is visible above the ground. But the crypts that he constructed under the high altars of both his basilicas, to house precious relics, have survived (figs.48,49,51). Each has a main chamber (in which the relics were displayed) that was lit by lamps set in small niches in the walls. Those wishing to view the relics would have entered the crypt by means of steep stone staircases leading to darkened, narrow winding passages which opened into the central (lighted) chamber.

A number of sculptural fragments have also survived which provide a clear indication of the impressive, Gallic and Roman, character of Wilfrid's Northumbrian foundations. Architectural fragments carved with animals and small figures set in elaborate vinescrolls recall similar schemes decorating churches in Rome; a large sunburst reproduces a carving set over the entrance to a church in Poitiers. The remains of two cross-shafts, dated to the first half of the eighth century, and perhaps produced during the abbacy of Acca (Wilfrid's successor at Hexham) have also survived. These are decorated with elaborate vinescroll motifs and an image of the Crucifixion copied from a very early Christian model probably imported from Rome.

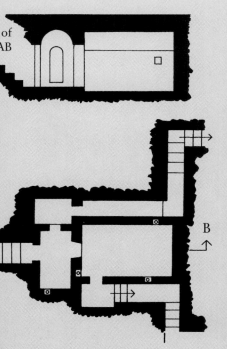

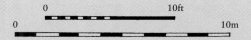

0   10ft

0   10m

fig.49 - Plan and elevation of the crypt built by Wilfrid under his church at Hexham.
After Taylor and Taylor 1978.

The Glory of the Church

Although they functioned as courts in many respects, the monasteries of Anglo-Saxon Northumbria were also centres of religion and education. Their wealth was not lavished solely on secular concerns. Large investments were also made in constructing and decorating the buildings which represented the institution of the Church.

At the most prestigious centres stone churches were built. In a landscape filled with settlements made of wood and thatch, wattle and daub, these buildings would have been impressive in the extreme. And they were intended to impress. One of the first to be built, by Wilfrid at Hexham, had columns and side aisles, a crypt (*fig.51*), stairs and passages. For Wilfrid's biographer, Eddius Stephanus, there was no finer church outside Italy (*Life of Wilfrid* ch.22).

This was not simply rhetorical praise on Eddius' part, for it was from Italy and Gaul, from the Church of Rome, that men like Wilfrid deliberately sought inspiration for the churches that they erected in the Northumbrian countryside. When Benedict Biscop, who had accompanied Wilfrid on his first journey to Italy, decided to build stone churches for his monastic foundations at Jarrow (*fig.50*) and

fig.50 - The church of St Paul at Jarrow, Tyne & Wear, with its 7th- century Anglo-Saxon chancel originally built as a separate chapel.

fig.51 - The crypt built by Wilfrid at Hexham, Northumberland, in about 672.

Wearmouth, he deliberately brought in masons and glaziers from Gaul. These were men who could build in (what Bede describes as) "the Roman style": in stone, as opposed to the wood and thatch used to construct the churches of the Irish monastic centres like that at Lindisfarne (*Lives of the Abbots* ch.5).

In their general layout and appearance these churches (at Hexham, Jarrow and Wearmouth) did, indeed, replicate those found in Rome and Gaul at the time. They were, like churches such as Sta Maria Cosmedin in Rome, basilican-style structures. They had long, high, narrow naves which were lit by small round-headed windows set high up in the walls. Single-storied chambers (porticus) or aisles ran along each side. A small chancel was set at the eastern end, and at the western end was an entrance porch. Even the Roman custom of prominently displaying the dedication of the church was imitated by Benedict Biscop at Jarrow, with the dedication stone recording the name and date of his original church (*fig.52*).

The impressive effect achieved by such constructions was not limited to the stone churches, however; many of the other buildings in the 'Roman' monastic complexes were also built of stone. To the south of the main basilica at Jarrow were structures housing the abbot, the refectory and dormitory of the monastery. The principal monastic buildings were built of stone with plastered walls and ornate floors, and they were set with coloured glass windows.

fig.52 - Dedication stone at Jarrow, recording the date of Benedict Biscop's foundation of the church in 685.

Other, smaller churches were also erected in these centres. The remains of three such buildings have been identified at Hexham, while at Jarrow, the chancel of the present building was originally a separate chapel which stood to the east of the main basilica. Standing almost in its entirety this building gives us a good idea of the defining characteristics of the impressive stone churches of Anglo-Saxon Northumbria: tall, narrow dimensions; very large, roughly cut quoin stones set at the corners of the buildings; walls approximately 76 cm (2ft 6in) thick; massive 'through stones' (single stones which pass through the thickness of the wall) used in the construction of the windows and doors; and distinctive small, round-headed windows set high up in the walls.

The access to stone and labour required to construct such churches and monastic complexes meant that not many were built. Wood remained the primary building material for Anglo-Saxon ecclesiastical centres. But, other stone churches were built, most notably at Escomb in County Durham where the present parish church represents one of the few near-complete Anglo-Saxon churches left in England (*fig.59*). Like the small chapel at Jarrow, it has all the distinctive features which identify churches that were originally Anglo-Saxon foundations even where later additions have intruded into the Anglo-Saxon fabric, as is the case at St Peter's, Bywell (Northumberland), or Ledsham in Yorkshire.

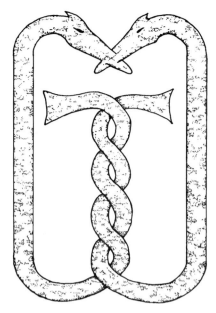

fig.53 - Serpents carved on the late 7th-century portal stones of the church at Monkwearmouth; the tails are twisted together to form a Tau-shaped cross.

fig.54 - Fragment of an early 8th-century architectural frieze from the Anglo-Saxon church at Jarrow; a shield-bearing warrior and a small beast can be seen in the vinescroll motif.

St. Paul's Church, Jarrow, Tyne & Wear.

WEARMOUTH AND JARROW

The twin monasteries of Wearmouth and Jarrow, founded by Benedict Biscop in 674 and 681 respectively, are probably the best-known of all ecclesiastical foundations in Anglo-Saxon England. The details of their early history, provided in two contemporary accounts: Bede's History of the Abbots *and an anonymous* Life of Ceolfrith, *the first abbot of Jarrow, have been well supplemented by excavations that have revealed many of the original monastic buildings. Together these sources indicate that the overall community was extremely large and rich. The endowments made by Ecgfrith and other members of the Northumbrian aristocracy totalled about 150*

fig.55 - Benedict Biscop's Church of St Pe[...] Monkwearmouth, showing the Anglo-Sax[...] tower and part of the original west wall.

hides of land. One hide was the amount of land deemed sufficient to sustain a freeman and his family, along with those who worked it. It could vary from 60-120 acres, depending on the locality. When Ceolfrith departed for Rome in 716 the Wearmouth-Jarrow estate supported nearly 700 monks.

At the centre of the landed estates were the monastic buildings themselves, buildings which were designed to replicate those seen by Benedict Biscop in Gaul and Italy. The churches were built of stone, set with coloured glass windows and very richly decorated. Paintings were brought from Rome and hung in the church at Wearmouth, elaborately carved stone friezes were set around the walls, and on the altar were vessels made of precious metals imported from Gaul.

The standing and archaeological remains amply confirm the sophistication of these buildings. The present west front of St Peter's, Monkwearmouth (fig.55), shows that Benedict's church was approximately 5m wide x 15m high (18 x 50ft), with a two-storied entrance porch which was heightened in the tenth century; the nave probably extended some 19.5m (64ft) in length. The church at Jarrow was even larger, being 27m long and nearly 6m wide (90 x 19ft). To the east of each church smaller chapels were erected, and to the south were the monastic buildings. These were built of stone, with floors of pounded tile, walls of painted plaster and windows set with coloured glass. They, too, were buildings of some considerable size: the refectory and chapter-house at Jarrow were 8m (26ft) wide by 27m (90ft) and 18m (60ft) long, respectively (fig.85).

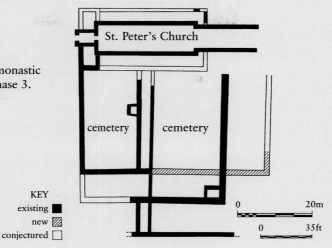

- Plan of the Anglo-Saxon monastic
lex of Wearmouth. Saxon Phase 3.
, J. Cramp 1984.

KEY
existing ■
new ▨
conjectured ▢

Nothing remains of the library so carefully built up by Benedict, but the extent of Bede's works provides some indication of its range, while the survival of the Codex Amiatinus, known to have been written at Wearmouth-Jarrow, means other manuscripts can be ascribed to the same scriptorium: including two copies of Bede's Ecclesiastical History, *which are now kept in Cambridge (the 'Moore Bede') and St Petersburg (the 'Leningrad Bede'), both of which have been dated to the early decades of the eighth century; the small St Cuthbert Gospel of St John, which was found among St Cuthbert's relics; and a part of the eighth-century 'Durham Gospels' kept in the cathedral library there.*

The reputation of Benedict and his monastery was widespread, and not simply in Northumbria. It was to Benedict that Adamnan, the abbot of Iona, turned when he considered converting to Roman orthodoxy in 688. In 710, when the Picts were seeking to establish friendly relations with Northumbria, they sent an embassy to Jarrow requesting instruction on the disputed issues of Easter and the tonsure, and architects to build a stone church in the Roman style.

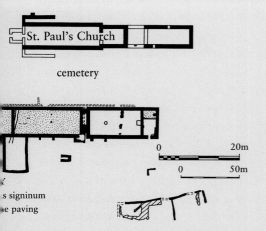

fig.57 - Plans of the Anglo-Saxon monastic complex of Jarrow.
After R. J. Cramp 1984.

BENEDICT BISCOP (628-690)

Benedict Biscop (Bishop) was one of the founding members of the Roman Church in Northumbria. Until the age of 25 he was a member of Oswiu's household, but in 653 he renounced secular life and, with Wilfrid, embarked on a pilgrimage to Rome. In 664 he determined to return, with Alhfrith, but Oswiu intervened and Benedict travelled alone, first to Rome and then to Lérins, an island monastery off the south coast of Gaul, where he took his monastic vows. From there he returned to Rome in 667, intending to remain permanently. But when he arrived, Wigheard, who had come to Rome to be installed as archbishop of Canterbury, died of the plague. Benedict was asked to escort the new archbishop, Theodore of Tarsus, and his North African companion, Hadrian, back to England. Arriving in 669, Benedict remained in Canterbury until 671 when he travelled to Rome for the fourth time - to obtain books. More were collected on his last two visits (in 678-80 and 684-7), along with paintings and relics.

Oswiu had died in 670, removing any royal antagonism towards Benedict over his friendship with Alhfrith. Thus, when Benedict came back to England he returned to Northumbria and devoted the remainder of his life to establishing a monastery. The first part of his foundation was built at the mouth of the River Wear, on land granted by Ecgfrith in 674. Its church was erected by artisans brought over from Gaul, its library was stocked with the books Benedict had acquired from Rome, the monks were trained in the liturgy by Abbot John, the archcantor of St Peter's in Rome, and in 678 the foundation was granted papal immunity from outside interference. Benedict had enjoyed good relations with Ecgfrith, but Wilfrid's problems at the time probably encouraged him to seek this privilege.

In 681 Ecgfrith made another donation of land, at Jarrow, for Benedict's second foundation; the church was dedicated in 685. A year later the community was struck by the plague and all the monks, except the abbot (Ceolfrith) and a young boy (thought to have been Bede), died. They were soon replaced, however, and the monastic complex became one of the largest in early medieval England.

Benedict himself died in 690 requesting that his Rule should be adhered to. It was based on the customs of 17 different European monasteries that Benedict had visited during his travels. He was also concerned that his library should be kept intact. Above all, he insisted that his monastery should be ruled by abbots elected on grounds of ability, not because of their relationship to him. This was in marked contrast to both Hild's and Wilfrid's institutions where the principle of hereditary succession was established by the founders, and indicates the value Benedict placed on learning and spirituality in monastic life.

fig.58 - Panel from an early 8th-century shrine decorated with the 'inhabited' vinescroll motif, from Jedburgh Abbey, The Borders.

Jedburgh Abbey Museum.

fig.59 - The 7th-century Anglo-Saxon stone church at Escomb, Co. Durham.

It was not merely the fact that monastic centres and churches like these were built of stone which made them so impressive in the Anglo-Saxon landscape, however. Significant investments were also made in their decoration. Stone sculpture was used, both outside and inside. A large zoomorphic sundial is set in the south wall of the church at Escomb. Intricately carved jambs and imposts adorned the entrances to the churches at Lastingham and Ledsham (Yorkshire). The exterior walls of the church porch at Wearmouth were decorated with a carved string course, and, set under the gable roof of the porch was a large, full-length statue. It is now too weathered to identify, but it would have represented either Christ or St Peter, to whom the church is dedicated. The porch was further decorated with two pairs of intertwining serpents, their tails twisted together to form a Tau-shaped cross (*fig.53*).

Inside, the walls were decorated with stone friezes carved with geometric, animal and floral motifs (*fig.54*). Again in imitation of the Roman churches, sculptured stone screens separated the altar at the east end of the church from the area of the nave; fragments of such a structure survive from the church at Jarrow.

A stone seat, carved with lions, was used at Wearmouth and at Hexham the bishop was enthroned in a monolithic stone chair (*fig.60*) similar to episcopal thrones used in churches in Gaul. In a number of churches elaborately carved shrines were set up, as at (*fig.58*) Jedburgh (Borders) and Hovingham (North Yorkshire).

These interior decorations were further accentuated by wall paintings and the brightly coloured light coming through the glass windows. A series of large paintings illustrating events from the bible was imported from Rome and set up in the church at Wearmouth, and at Escomb traces of plaster painted with a sinuous floral motif still survive in the chancel arch.

fig.60 - The late 7th-century bishop's throne from Wilfrid's foundation at Hexham, Northumberland.

Hexham Abbey.

In these buildings no expense was spared in the effort to reproduce the visible hallmarks of the rich and powerful Church of Rome, re-established in Anglo-Saxon Northumbria in the second half of the seventh century. Precious metals and gems were used to make the vessels needed for everyday worship: chalices, plates, covers and containers for manuscripts and relics; altars were covered with sheets of beaten silver and gold, studded with precious stones. Carved book covers, caskets and liturgical combs were made from bone. Expensive imported silks and finely woven and embroidered hangings were hung in the churches and used for the vestments worn by the priests officiating at the services (*fig.61*). The embroideries produced in England were so highly valued that they were exported to be worn by churchmen in Gaul and Italy in the eighth century; a bishop in Ravenna, for instance, was buried in robes decorated with strips of Anglo-Saxon embroidery.

And then there were the manuscripts. Some, undecorated, were made for use in the monastic libraries. Others, large and elaborately decorated, were carried in processions on religious feast-days and displayed on the high altar of the church.

fig.61 - Embroidered textile now at Maaseik in Belgium, showing the intricate and elaborate quality of Anglo-Saxon needlework; made in about 800.

St Catherina, Maaseik, Belgium.

But each manuscript, regardless of its purpose, required the skins of animals (calves and sheep) for their parchment or vellum pages. The process was long and involved a great deal of painstaking labour: each skin had to be soaked in a lime solution to loosen the hair and flesh, then stretched, scraped, washed and dried, and rubbed with pumice before it was ready to be used for writing on. And the number of skins needed was considerable: over 1,500 hides were used to make three complete bibles at Jarrow in the early eighth century.

The inks and paints used to embellish the parchment pages also had to be made from natural ingredients. They were extracted from plants, shellfish, and minerals, some of which were imported; one particular blue paint, for instance, was made from lapis lazuli brought ultimately from Afghanistan. Quill and reed pens and brushes had to be manufactured. Men and women had to spend months, even years, copying out the texts of the manuscripts and, where appropriate, decorating them. Covers had to be constructed from wood and leather and sometimes decorated with precious metals, gems and carved bone. Considered as manufactured artefacts, the manuscripts of the Northumbrian Church represent a considerable investment in valuable resources of land, animals, luxury imported goods, time and labour.

Manuscripts made in the Northumbrian monasteries cannot, however, be regarded as simply the products of investment in precious resources. Many were integral to the daily act of Christian worship and they were an essential part of the learning and scholarship fostered in the centres. From his early childhood, the monastery at Jarrow was the home of Bede, one of the leaders of Northumbrian academic life. The list of his works is impressive by any standard: in addition to his *Ecclesiastical History*, he produced over forty works explaining the text of the Bible, two books of homilies and sermons, books about the saints and martyrs of the Church, a history of the abbots of Jarrow and Wearmouth, books of poetry, hymns, literary theory, grammar and science. His histories are among the first to calculate time according to the 'Anno Domini' method, and his scientific treatises were some of the first in Western Europe to explain the workings of the moon on the tides. His influence on subsequent generations of scholars throughout the medieval period was enormous. His works were widely translated and circulated throughout Europe, and today his *Ecclesiastical History* alone survives in over 160 medieval manuscripts.

The monastic schools, which taught people like Bede, had access to a wide range of literature imported from Gaul and Italy. Men like Wilfrid and Biscop returned from their trips to Rome with all types of manuscripts to fill their schools and libraries. These provided the students with text-books, and the scribes with exemplars to copy and distribute to other centres. In the late eighth century the

THE CUTHBERT RELICS

In 698, when the monks of Lindisfarne decided to transfer Cuthbert's remains from the sarcophagus in which his body had been placed eleven years earlier, into a shrine which could be properly venerated, they discovered the body was still intact. Enshrined in a carved wooden chest in the sanctuary, it became the focus of one of the most famous pilgrimage centres in Anglo-Saxon England (fig.62).

So important was it, that when the monks left Lindisfarne in 875 they took Cuthbert's remains with them and re-established the shrine at Chester-le-Street where they settled in 883. It went with them when they moved yet again to Durham in 995. There it attracted pilgrims and wealth, making the Durham community one of the most powerful in England. In 1104 the shrine was opened before it was re-dedicated in the new Norman cathedral, but after that it lay undisturbed until 1539 when Henry VIII dissolved the monasteries. Then the shrine was destroyed and many of the valuables it had acquired were removed.

fig.62 - The wooden reliquary coffin of St Cuthbert, probably made in 698.

Durham Cathedral Treasury.

In 1827 the grave in which Cuthbert's body was thought to have been re-buried, was opened. It was at this point that the surviving relics were discovered. There were three coffins, the innermost made of wood incised with images of Christ and the four evangelist symbols on the lid, the archangels Michæl and Gabriel at one end and the Virgin and Child at the other, and the twelve apostles and five more archangels ranged along each side (fig.65). Inside, wrapped in many layers of cloth were Cuthbert's remains. Round his neck was a gold pectoral cross set with garnets and white shell inlay (fig.38). There was also an ivory comb, a portable wooden altar covered with silver (fig.32), and numerous pieces of rich textiles. Apart from the textiles, which were placed in the coffin during the later Anglo-Saxon period, all the other items are thought to be those buried

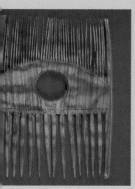

- Cuthbert's 7th-century
cal comb, made from
nt ivory.
a Cathedral Library.

with Cuthbert in 698 - as was a small gospel manuscript (the St Cuthbert Gospel of St John) which had been removed in 1104 (fig.64).

These objects are unique in many ways. The cross is the only such piece to have survived, complete, from the North of England; the coffin is the only substantial item of decorated woodwork to have emerged from the Anglo-Saxon period; the comb and altar are without parallel in early Anglo-Saxon England; and the gospel book is the earliest European manuscript to have survived in its original binding.

Furthermore, these artefacts reveal the high standard of craftsmanship attained by Northumbrian artists of all media and, more importantly, their decoration indicates just how widespread were the cultural contacts of the Lindisfarne community, as well as the extraordinary ability of the artists to assimilate and redefine their source material.

The comb is of elephant ivory imported from Africa; the central shell of the cross came from as far away as the Red Sea or Indian Ocean; the central motif on the front cover of the book derives ultimately from Coptic (Egyptian) art; while the coffin and altar look to Ireland, Gaul, Italy and the Middle East for their inspiration.

The practice of enshrining the remains of venerated churchmen in wooden coffins, lightly engraved with figural motifs, was introduced to Anglo-Saxon England from Gaul, while the models lying behind the figures came from the Mediterranean world of Italy and the Middle East. The choice of which archangels to portray, however, came from Ireland where they were included in the liturgy of the Church long after they had been abandoned elsewhere; the runic alphabet used to label the figures on the lid was drawn from Anglo-Saxon culture.

The extent to which these diverse traditions were used to create something new is best illustrated in the images of the Evangelist symbols set round the figure of Christ on the lid of the coffin. These are winged and haloed full-length symbols, holding books. As such they are a type which was to become common throughout Europe, but in Mediterranean art until that time the symbols were usually portrayed as half-length creatures with wings, haloes and books. In Ireland, by contrast, it is thought that the symbols were (as in the Book of Durrow) full-length figures with no attributes (no haloes, wings or books). On the Cuthbert coffin the two traditions have been brought together to produce a new, composite image.

fig.64 - Original leather binding of the St Cuthbert Gospel of St John taken from the saint's coffin; produced in about 698 at Wearmouth-Jarrow.

On loan to the British Library.

library at York contained works by Greek and Roman philosophers, herbalists and gardeners. There were histories and political treatises, books of classical poetry, works by writers of the Christian Church (including those of "Master Bede"), and books of grammar and rhetoric: "A multitude of works of scholarship" (*The Saints of the Church of York* l.1559).

Although such scholarship was conducted in Latin, the Anglo-Saxon churchmen did not neglect their own language, English. In fact, the origins of English literature can be traced to one of the Northumbrian monasteries: Whitby. Until the seventh century no attempt was made to preserve the oral poetry of the Anglo-Saxon scops; it was regarded by the Church as irredeemably 'heathen'. But, in the last decades of the seventh century, Cædmon, a labourer on the monastic estate of Whitby who was apparently unable to sing or recite the traditional poetry of the Anglo-Saxons, had a vision in which he acquired, not only these skills, but also the ability to transform such poetry into the service of the Church. He gained the ability to compose songs in the manner of the Anglo-Saxon scops - as a series of short alliterating phrases - but instead of using such phrases to recite 'heathen' heroic epics, he was inspired to turn them to Christian subject-matter. With his new-found skills Cædmon entered the monastery of Whitby and spent the rest of his life dictating English poems on biblical subjects to the monks who recorded them (*Ecclesiastical History* IV, 24).

In much of the English poetry which was subsequently produced in the monasteries the heroes of Anglo-Saxon verse were replaced by saints and biblical figures who acted much as their heroic predecessors had done. Christ, in the Old English poem 'The Dream of the Rood', for instance, is presented as a princely warrior who battles with Death. Instead of dying as a sacrificial victim, however, Christ in this poem strides onto the battlefield, strips himself in preparation for combat, and in death merely rests, weary after the conflict. In keeping with this rendition of the story, the cross of the crucifixion is presented as his thane who is eventually rewarded for his loyal service with gold and precious gems.

The more elegiac secular poetry of the Anglo-Saxons was also employed by the Christian poets. Bede himself is credited with the composition of just such a poem:

> Before the inevitable journey no one can be
> So wise that for him it will not be necessary
> To consider, before his going hence,
> What, for his soul, of good or ill,
> After his death-day, the judgement will be.

Known as 'Bede's Death Song', this poem is composed of the phrases characteristic of Anglo-Saxon poetry and it evokes very succinctly the notions of transience associated with this life which is found so often in the pre-Christian poetry. But, one of Bede's pupils records that the subject-matter of this poem was in fact inspired by a passage from the Bible (Paul's Letter to the Hebrews 10, 27). Thus, with this short verse we have the intricate fusion of two different literary cultures: the secular poetics of the Anglo-Saxons and the subject-matter of Christianity, the two serving to reinforce each other, and at the same time produce something new and distinctively different from the two traditions which inspired it.

fig.65 - Drawing showing a reconstruction of the images of Christ and the four Evangelist symbols incised on the lid of St Cuthbert's coffin.

Durham Cathedral Treasury.

fig.66 - The York Helmet, from the
Coppergate excavations in York; second
half of the 8th century.

York Castle Museum.

The Art of the Golden Age

The fusion of cultural traditions (Christian and secular Anglo-Saxon) found in the poetry is also one of the defining characteristics of the visual arts produced in Northumbria between the late seventh and early ninth centuries.

The eighth-century helmet from Coppergate in York, for instance, combines Christian with secular Anglo-Saxon motifs in its use of boar-heads and a serpent whose body is filled with an inscription invoking the protection of God (*fig.66*). The serpent motif had long been used in the decoration of weapons and belt-buckles worn by Anglo-Saxon warriors and in such contexts probably had a strongly protective function. On this helmet, however, the serpent's body is arranged so that it incorporates a cross over the crown of the helmet. The inscription makes the implied Christian symbolism explicit.

The gold filigree decoration of the late seventh-century Hunterston brooch, on the other hand, appropriates motifs familiar to the repertoire of (pre-Christian) Anglo-Saxon metalwork, and re-defines them as Christian symbols (*fig.67*). The Irish penannular form of the brooch itself incorporates the shape of a tiny manuscript set among intricate filigree patterns of interlaced animals with pairs of curve-beaked birds of prey which peck at tiny gold beads on its edges. Together

fig.67 - The Hunterston brooch, with its minute 'manuscript' and bird motif; late 7th - early 8th century. *National Museums of Scotland.*

fig.68 - Portrait of the Old Testament scribe Ezra, from the Codex Amiatinus 1,fV., produced at the Wearmouth-Jarrow scriptorium sometime before 716.

fig.69 - The uncial script used for the text of the Codex Amiatinus 1, f.9v.
Biblioteca Medicea Laurenziana, Florence, Italy.

with the minute 'manuscript' these birds function as Christian symbols: feeding off 'berries' set round the 'manuscript' they are symbolic of living creatures receiving sustenance from 'The Book of Life'. And, difficult as it is to decipher, the scheme not only presents a coherent Christian image, it also hides a minute container for a holy relic. Yet, when worn none of this could have been visible under the pin holding the brooch to the robe.

It is not only the decoration of 'secular' artefacts such as helmets and brooches which reveal the cultural fusion and evolution of the different artistic traditions circulating in Northumbria from the later seventh century onwards. Specifically religious objects, such as the manuscripts and stone carvings, also incorporate the motifs and decorative schemes from the various art styles: the Germanic art of the Anglo-Saxons and the Christian art of Ireland was supplemented by that of the Mediterranean world and Gaul.

Artefacts imported from Italy by Augustine's mission in the late sixth century and by Anglo-Saxon churchmen a century later, were decorated in the tradition inherited by Christian artists of the Mediterranean from the world of late antiquity: the art of imperial Rome based on naturalistic representations of plants, animals and the human form. In the manuscripts the Evangelists (the writers of the Gospels) were portrayed seated on stools, pens in their hands, books or scrolls open on their knees, and the tools of their trade by their side (*fig.68*). The faces and bodies of the figures set in such detailed surroundings were carefully modelled with shading and highlights.

The imported Italian manuscripts also introduced the Northumbrian artists and scribes to another script: the 'uncial script', a rounded and very formal script distinguished from the half uncial by its use of many capital letter-forms. It was the script which had been used in Italian scriptoria for biblical texts since the fourth century (*fig.69*).

It was through such artefacts that the Northumbrian artists became acquainted with a fully developed system of symbolic images used to convey the notions central to Christianity. The Evangelist portraits, for example, were accompanied by winged creatures (an ox, lion, eagle and man) considered to symbolise the divine text of their gospels. The grape-vine was another popular symbol which, inspired by a passage in the Bible (*John 15, 1*) where Christ describes himself as the "True Vine", conveyed a complex set of ideas. It represented Christ, his Church on earth, and the sacraments of that Church. Ultimately it could represent the eternal life available through faith in Christ and his sacraments.

In some cases the decorated artefacts imported from the Mediterranean and Gaul were faithfully reproduced by the Northumbrian scribes and artists. A small silver plaque from Hexham depicts, in simple outline, a saint holding a book. The closest parallels in style and technique are found in the art of seventh- and eighth-century Gaul. The plaque reflects the strong influence of the Gallic Church on men like Wilfrid (*fig.70*).

Manuscripts were also made to replicate their Mediterranean exemplars. The Codex Amiatinus (now in Florence), one of three bibles produced at the Wearmouth-Jarrow scriptorium, reproduces the uncial script and decoration of sixth-century Italian manuscript art so carefully that for many centuries it was believed to be an Italian book; it was only at the end of the nineteenth century that the bible was recognised as having been written in Northumbria in the early years of the eighth century under the guidance of Ceolfrith, the first abbot of Jarrow.

fig.70 - 8th-century silver plaque from Hexham. The design and figural style were influenced by Gallic art of the period.
British Museum.

fig.71 - Prologue and contents of the Codex Amiatinus 1, f.IV; written on a page of parchment dyed purple and using gold leaf in the decoration.

Biblioteca Medicea Laurenziana, Florence, Italy.

fig.72 - Portrait of the Evangelist Matthew, from the Lindisfarne Gospels, f.25b; written at Lindisfarne, Holy Island, Northumberland in about 698.

British Library.

Apart from faithfully reproducing the sixth-century Italian uncial script, the Codex Amiatinus also bears many of the hallmarks of Italian manuscript art in its decoration. A number of its pages are dyed purple and written on in gold and silver, features common to early Italian (particularly imperial) manuscripts. Its canon tables (lists of equivalent passages found in the four gospels) are arranged in architectural arcades as they were in Italian manuscripts. In the Irish-influenced Book of Durrow these lists were arranged simply in blocks. The figural decoration of the Codex Amiatinus is also fully representational: the figures are modelled with highlights and shading, they are realistically clothed and their surroundings are in full perspective.

The degree to which this manuscript reproduces its Italian exemplars is perhaps an indicator of the extent to which the founders of the Wearmouth-Jarrow monastery valued the trappings of the Roman Church. It certainly reveals the extent to which Northumbrian artists could be influenced by Mediterranean work. But other Northumbrian artists and craftsmen were less concerned to produce such close copies of their models. More characteristic was the tendency to appropriate the motifs and symbols of Italian and Gallic art and fuse them with the decorative techniques of the Irish Church and their own, native Anglo-Saxon art. As a result, naturalistic representations of the human form were

fig.73 - Carpet page preceding the Gospel of St Mark in the Lindisfarne Gospels, f.94b.

British Library.

THE LINDISFARNE GOSPELS

The Lindisfarne Gospels, more than any other single artefact, has come to be identified with the Golden Age of Northumbria. The sumptuously decorated pages define what is commonly known as 'insular manuscript art', and, just as importantly, the manuscript can be identified with the cradle of Northumbrian Christianity: Lindisfarne.

A colophon (short end note) added to the manuscript in the late tenth century, attributes the production of the book to Eadfrith (the first known English artist) who became bishop of Lindisfarne in 698, shortly after the transfer of Cuthbert's remains. Indeed, the Gospels are usually understood to have been prepared for that occasion.

As one of the definitive pieces of insular manuscript art the Lindisfarne Gospels reveals the influence and transformation of the various artistic traditions circulating in Northumbria at the time: Italian, Irish and Anglo-Saxon. The influence of Italian work is evident in the gospel text. Set out in two columns, as in late antique Mediterranean manuscripts, it was apparently copied from a book which had at some stage passed through a Neapolitan scriptorium. The script (fig.74), however, is the half uncial script introduced to Northumbria from the Irish scriptoria.

Almost every part of the Lindisfarne Gospels displays this process of amalgamation and subsequent transformation of different artistic traditions. The canon tables (fig.75) are arranged in the arcades of the Italian manuscripts, but instead of the columns being painted as architectural features, they are treated as long thin panels of decoration, filled with geometric and interlace motifs, and surrounded by minute red dots.

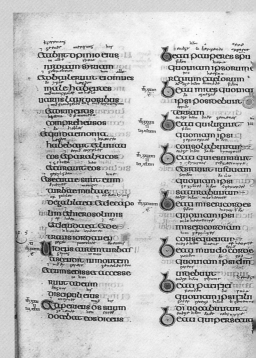

fig.74 - The text of the Lindisfarne Gospels, se in two columns of insular half-uncial script; in minuscule has been used for the interlinear glo f.34.

British Library.

90

Irish, Anglo-Saxon and Mediterranean influences are identifiable, but the way they have been brought together transforms them into a new and individual art.

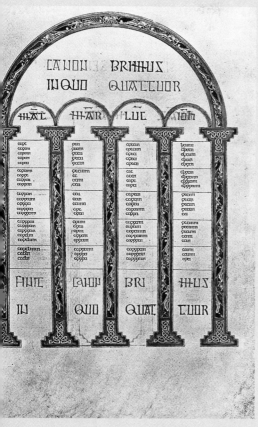

The portraits of the Evangelists were also derived from Mediterranean exemplars. The image of Matthew (fig.72) was in fact taken from the same south Italian model as a portrait of the scribe Ezra illustrated in the Codex Amiatinus (fig.68). But whereas the artist of the Wearmouth-Jarrow manuscript was concerned to reproduce his Mediterranean model as closely as possible, Eadfrith used it as a starting point to produce something very different. His figure of Matthew has been removed from the surroundings so realistically portrayed in the Codex Amiatinus and set on a plain white background. Notions of roundness, solidity and perspective have all been replaced with highly coloured and flat, patterned shapes contained within bold dark outlines. It is a distinctive treatment used for all the portraits of the Evangelists.

- Canon tables in the Lindisfarne Gospels, f.11.
..ibrary.

The decorated initial letters (figs.2,76) inspired by Irish manuscript art are also present in the Lindisfarne Gospels but here they do not have the same relationship with the following text as they do in earlier manuscripts. The whole page is framed, and the words following the initial letter are arranged round it; the initial letter has been transformed into a 'picture' whose function is to announce the opening of the gospel. The page has to be turned to discover what the text actually says.

And, there are the carpet pages(fig.73). As in the earlier Book of Durrow these are pages full of decorative motifs: Celtic spiral, pelta and trumpet designs mingle with Anglo-Saxon interlace and animal patterns. But in the Lindisfarne Gospels these pages present dominant cross-shapes. Although formed from panels of zoomorphic and geometric patterns, the crosses fill and quarter the pages.

✠ lucas uitulus ⁊
on gynned   god ꞃpell
incipit euangelium   secundum lucam

QUO
NIAM
                    aᴇᴄ   ꞃoð
QUIDE✠
          moniᵹo   cunnᴇnðo
MULTICOᴺᴬ
          poᵹꞃon   þᴇꞇᴜ ᵹᴇ
LISUNTORDINA
      ᴇnðoᵹꞃᴇðnᴜðon   ꞃᴜꞇ ᵹᴇꞃᴀᵹᴀ
RENARRATIONEM

transformed under the influence of curvilinear, geometric, and zoomorphic patterns. The same pictorial schemes were illustrated, but they were transfigured by the dictates of pattern, line and colour.

In the portraits of the Evangelists found in the Northumbrian manuscripts, for instance, perspective disappears. The stools and thrones become broad bands of bright colour sometimes ending in beast-heads, and are filled with intricate patterns. The figures are stylised, their clothing flattened by the effect of hard outlines and contrasting colours used to indicate folds. In some manuscripts the Evangelists are accompanied by their winged symbols, but in others they are completely replaced by the beasts. When arcades are used to surround the canon tables the architectural columns are treated as long thin fields of geometric and zoomorphic ornament.

The decorative techniques originally introduced through the Irish centres also evolved dramatically during this period as the Northumbrian artists grew more familiar with the potential of their designs. The carpet pages in the Lindisfarne Gospels teem with zoomorphic, interlace and curvilinear motifs; pairs of confronting beasts overflow the frames to crouch on the outer borders, much as they do on the edges of Anglo-Saxon brooches. And, despite the apparently overwhelming desire of the artists to fill the entire page with these decorative motifs, they are systematically arranged so that the shape of the cross is presented, sometimes repeatedly, between them (fig.73).

The decorated initials are also enlarged and extended. In the Lindisfarne Gospels they fill the page, leaving little space for the text immediately following the opening words of the passage. Here again the curving patterns of the Celtic world appear side by side with the interlace and animal ornament of the Anglo-Saxons, distorting the shape of the letters. The text which remains on these 'initial pages' is also decorated, the letters being filled with blocks of colour, minute interlace patterns, and small beast-heads. The red dots, used to highlight them further, also form interlace patterns and animals whose bodies are entwined between the letters (fig.76).

What were, in the Italian and early Irish and Northumbrian manuscripts, methods of arranging the text, of marking the opening of a passage or a significant part of the text, have become pages devoted to an abundance of colour and ornament.

Carved artefacts produced in Northumbria in the later seventh and eighth centuries also reveal the characteristic tendency to fuse and transform the various

fig.76 - Initial page of the Gospel of St Luke, from the Lindisfarne Gospels, f.139.
British Library.

THE FRANKS CASKET

fig.77 - Front panel of the Franks Casket, illustrating the story of Weland the Smith and the Adoration of the Christ Child by the Three Magi.
British Museum.

The fusion of old and new, pagan and Christian, Germanic and Mediterranean, so definitive of the art of the Golden Age of Northumbria, is nowhere more evident than in the decoration of the Franks Casket (figs.77-79) which was made in Northumbria in about 700. This remarkable item is covered with scenes illustrating events from Germanic legend, Roman mythology, Jewish history and Christian tradition. Inscriptions, using both the runic and Latin alphabets, identify each image. The casket itself is bordered by a runic inscription telling how it was made from the bones of a whale stranded on the beach.

The influence of the Mediterranean world lies behind the construction of the casket and in the way the decoration is arranged (both of which mimic the sarcophagi and reliquary caskets of Italy), and in a number of the figural scenes. Romulus and Remus the founders of ancient Rome, are illustrated on one side of the casket (fig.78) being nurtured in the woods by the wolf. On the lid is depicted the Sack of Jerusalem by the Romans. Inscriptions identify the battle, the glory of the victors, and the flight and captivity of the Jews.

These Mediterranean scenes, however, have been transformed in the hands of the Northumbrian artists. The image of Romulus and Remus retains few of the naturalistic features of classical art. The twins suckling the she-wolf defy gravity, while another wolf, escaping the hunters, flees through the undergrowth at the top of the picture. The hunters themselves are portrayed as Anglo-Saxons, as are many of the figures involved in the Sack of Jerusalem. In this latter image the runic inscriptions transport the action into the world of Anglo-Saxon England: the victorious Romans are labelled with the word 'DOM' (an extraordinarily resonant Old English word for 'glory' and 'power' or 'renown'), the qualities by which heroes in the poetry of the scops were judged.

The illustration on the front of the casket demonstrates a similar process of cultural eclecticism and assimilation (fig.77). On the right is a picture of the Magi adoring the Christ Child. The portrayal of the Virgin and Child derives ultimately from icons of the eastern Church of Byzantium which, in the seventh century, were fashionable in Rome. The three kings, however, are Anglo-Saxons, with their cloaks, tunics, leggings, long hair and beards. Here the world of the Anglo-Saxon north has been fused with that of the Mediterranean south in a most intricate way to produce a scene unique in the corpus of early Christian art - Germanic warrior kings pay homage to a Christ Child inspired by the art of the Mediterranean.

fig.78 - Side panel of the Franks Casket, illustrating the discovery of Romulus and Remus; 700-750.

British Museum.

Set beside this scene is a composite image illustrating events from the life of Weland the Smith, some of which are recounted in the Old English poem 'Deor'. It shows Weland, accompanied by Beaduhild (who stands behind him), offering his captor, Nithhad, a cup he has made from the skull of one of Nithhad's dead sons whose headless body lies at their feet. Weland is then depicted catching birds to make himself a flying machine from birds' wings in order to make good his escape. Here the techniques of narrative figural illustration, learnt from the art of the Christian Church, have been applied to native Germanic material. They are used elsewhere on the casket to illustrate other (unknown) events from Germanic legend: Egil the archer defending his home and 'Hos' seated on her 'sorrow-mound'.

influences circulating in the region during the 'Golden Age'. The Franks Casket , made of whale's bone in Northumbria in the first half of the eighth century is one such object (*figs.77-79*). Carved with scenes illustrating events from Roman mythology, Jewish history, Christian tradition and Anglo-Saxon legend it reveals the extraordinary eclectism of the Anglo-Saxon artists, and the extent to which they used the various models available to them as sources of mutual inspiration to produce an art definably different to the diverse styles which lay behind it.

Larger scale stone carvings demonstrate a similar process at work. Until the introduction of Roman Christianity and its culture, the Anglo-Saxons had never worked in stone. Their traditional materials were metal and wood. But, once the art of stone carving had been introduced into the region by craftsmen from Gaul the Northumbrians appropriated it and used it to create an entirely new art form: the High Cross. How and why this type of monument was developed is not known, but it may well have been another manifestation of the Northumbrian artists' ability to appropriate and assimilate the different cultural traditions available to them: in this case, the Irish tradition of raising wooden crosses which Oswald, for one, encountered on Iona; the suggested Anglo-Saxon tradition of erecting totem poles at sites of ritual importance, such as Yeavering; the Christian Mediterranean tradition of stone carving, introduced into the area in the later seventh century; and, the celebration of the Feast of the True Cross in the Anglo-Saxon Church after the discovery, in Rome, of fragments of the True Cross at the turn of the eighth century.

fig.79 -
The Franks Casket, carved in Northumbria from a whale's bone; about 700-750.
British Museum.

96

fig.80 - The west face of the
Bewcastle Cross shaft, Cumbria;
first half of the 8th century.

fig.81 - Cross shaft from Nunnykirk, Northumberland; all four faces of the monument are filled with different forms of the vinescroll motif; early 9th century.

Museum of Antiquities, University of Newcastle upon Tyne.

Whatever the inspiration for the stone crosses of Northumbria, from the first half of the eighth century increasing numbers of large, free-standing crosses, consisting of a slender shaft topped with a cross-head, were set up both inside churches and out in the countryside. They became perhaps the most important and abundant sculptural form in the North. Carved in relief on all four sides, they were originally painted and sometimes set with metal and paste glass. In many cases they replicated, in monumental form, the brilliant, gem-encrusted crosses made of precious metals which were carried in processions and set on the church altars. With some crosses standing up to 6m (20ft) tall they were highly visible reminders of the presence of the Church in the region, and seem to have been used not simply as memorials or objects of veneration, but also to mark meeting places, estate boundaries, and processional ways to churches.

The carved surfaces were filled with a great variety of decorative motifs: complex interlace patterns, pairs of confronting interlaced animals, panels replicating the work of jewellers, and above all, the vine-scroll. This motif was used so frequently to decorate the crosses it has become synonymous with them. It provided the sculptors with an almost infinite variety of forms: it could be naturalistic, winding its way up the shaft of the cross as a single-stemmed vine; it could be highly stylised, with the scrolls forming tight curls and the grapes, bulbous circles; it could grow up the length of the shaft as a double stem, with bunches of grapes contained in neat repeating medallions formed by the crossings of the stems; and it could be filled with small birds and animals, some naturalistic, some fantastic, feeding off the fruit. On the Nunnykirk Cross (*fig.81*), a different type of vine is used to fill each face of the shaft. In such cases the vine and cross work together as potent symbols of Christianity and its life-saving doctrines.

Figural scenes and portraits of Christ, his apostles, and the patrons of the Church, were also used to decorate the crosses. Such images were generally copied from artefacts imported from Italy and Gaul. On crosses like those from Easby, Otley and Collingham (Yorkshire), series of bust-length figures of the apostles fill the faces of the shaft. With their short hair and toga-like garments, they resemble, very closely, figures depicted in the work of late antiquity.

The narrative scenes carved on the crosses usually depict stories from the New Testament. The column at Masham (Yorkshire) contains some of the only Old Testament scenes to have survived (*fig.82*): David is illustrated slaying the lion and composing the psalms, and Samson is depicted carrying off the Gates of Gaza. The New Testament stories which were illustrated were also limited in their range, with the infancy and passion of Christ being portrayed more commonly than events from his ministry.

This selective use of narrative scenes was due to the fact that while such images illustrated stories, they were also understood to refer to other, doctrinal, matters: the sacraments of the Church, or the resurrection and salvation offered through Christianity. The Masham scene of Samson with the Gates of Gaza, for example, was understood to refer to Christ overcoming death, as the Gates of Gaza were equivalents of the Gates of Hell. Likewise, a carving of the Ascension of Christ, such as appears on the base of the Rothbury Cross, illustrates the moment of his Ascension into heaven accompanied by angels and watched by his apostles and the evangelists holding their gospel books. But it was also understood to portray the future Day of Judgement, when Christ would return with his angels to judge the human race, as foretold in the Gospels.

The motifs and figural images used to decorate the crosses were not chosen simply because they were available; they were selected for their relevant symbolic

value. The vine, because it could be employed to transform a stone cross into a physical representation of the Tree of Life, was used with great frequency on the stone monuments, but it was hardly ever used in the manuscripts. Images of the evangelists accompanied by their symbols, on the other hand, which are so common (as author portraits) in the gospel manuscripts, are extremely rare on the crosses.

Whatever the medium, the art of the Golden Age demonstrates the wide-ranging contacts of the Northumbrian Church and the use to which they were put in the hands of the artists. It also shows how well versed the patrons of the Golden Age arts were in Christian lore and doctrine. It is the art of a rich and learned culture.

fig.82 - The Masham column, North Yorkshire; early 9th century.

THREE NORTHUMBRIAN CROSSES -
BEWCASTLE, RUTHWELL AND ROTHBURY

The cross-shafts which stand at Ruthwell (Dumfries) and Bewcastle (Cumbria) are the most famous of the Anglo-Saxon stone crosses. They were probably among the first to be erected, in the first half of the eighth century. They have many distinctive features which they share with pieces of a late eighth century cross which once stood at Rothbury in Northumberland. This indicates that all three crosses were produced by the same 'school' of stone carvers which was probably based at Wearmouth-Jarrow.

In all respects these were impressive monuments. All three once stood over 5m (16ft) tall, and were carved on all four faces with geometric, vegetal and figural decoration. The eyes of the figures are still very deeply drilled, indicating that they would originally have been set with paste glass. Those at Ruthwell and Bewcastle were further ornamented with inscriptions in runes(used for Old English) and roman capitals (used for Latin). The Latin inscriptions identify many of the figural scenes, while the runes at Bewcastle record the names of those in whose memory the cross was erected. Unfortunately, they are so worn they can no longer be deciphered. At Ruthwell (fig.83), the runes record part of the Old English poem, 'The Dream Of The Rood'. Displaying this mixture of scripts the crosses are clearly products of the Northumbrian Golden Age.

fig.83 - The Ruthwell Cross Dumfries, with the inhabited vinescroll also found on the Bewcastle Cross, and the Old English poem 'The Dream of Rood' carved in runes in the borders; mid-8th century.

As such they also reveal the eclecticism of the Northumbrian artists, in this case applied to the monumental form of the High Cross. Drawn from the art of the Mediterranean world are the figures, with their short hair and togas, and the grape vines which fill two sides of the Ruthwell Cross and one side of both the Bewcastle and Rothbury Crosses. From the repertoire of the Anglo-Saxon artists came the panels of interlace and geometric patterns found at Bewcastle and Rothbury, and the fantastic creatures which fill the vines on all three Crosses - creatures whose tails evolve into the scrolls of the plant itself.

For all that these monuments emerged from the same centre of production and have so many features in common, they do, nevertheless, reveal significant differences in their function and decoration. The Rothbury Cross, for instance, was probably made to stand inside the church. Candles or lighted wicks were set in holes on the cross-arms. Those at Bewcastle and Ruthwell were erected outside.

Furthermore, the decoration of the Bewcastle Cross (fig.3,80) includes only three figural scenes, while there are at least nine on the Ruthwell Cross and seven still survive on the three remaining pieces of the Rothbury Cross. Of these scenes two occur at both Bewcastle and Ruthwell (John the Baptist, and Christ standing over two beasts). At Bewcastle they accompany a rare portrayal of a secular figure who holds a bird of prey. This may represent the man in whose honour the Cross was erected.

His presence (and the runic inscription) indicate that the Bewcastle Cross had a strongly commemorative function, in addition to any liturgical importance it had. The sundial on the south face would have called members of a monastic order to prayer, while the iconographic details of the biblical figures would have been understood to refer to the celebration of the Mass.

4 - Scene of the Damned in Hell,
:d on the late 8th-century
bury Cross shaft, which now
:s as the font base in Rothbury
ch, Northumberland.

The iconography of the figural scenes at Ruthwell indicate it too had a liturgical function. Here, however, such references (found in the images of John the Baptist, Christ, and the monastic saints Paul and Anthony shown breaking bread together) are supplemented by a number of scenes from the life of Christ. These refer to the manner in which Christians are saved through the sacraments of the Church.

The message of salvation is signified by many of the figural scenes which have survived at Rothbury, although here different images have been chosen for the purpose. The Raising of Lazarus, featured at the top of the shaft, has been used to symbolise the general resurrection of the dead at the end of time. The Ascension featured at the base is intended to recall the Day of Judgement, while another image on the base vividly portrays the Damned in Hell (fig.84) struggling in the coils of serpentine monsters which fill the panel. In the flickering light of the candles set on the cross-arms above, this image would have had a powerful effect on a viewer kneeling before the Cross inside the darkened church.

ALCUIN (c.735-804)

The son of a Bernician nobleman, Alcuin is remembered most as one of the leading figures of the Carolingian Renaissance for his work as a scholar and educational reformer in Gaul. He received his initial training in the monastic school at York founded by Egbert, one of Bede's pupils. In 767, when his master, Æthelberht, succeeded Egbert as archbishop of York, Alcuin took over the headship of the school, a post he held for the next thirteen years. During this period he made two journeys to Rome, and when Æthelberht resigned the see of York late in 780, Alcuin was sent again to Rome to acquire the pallium for the new archbishop.

It was on his return from this mission that Alcuin met Charlemagne and was offered a place at the Frankish court. In 782 he took up the position and became the head of the palace school at Aachen, chief adviser to Charlemagne on doctrinal issues, and his agent in all his dealings with the English (most notably in 786 and 790-3). He was rewarded, in 796, with the abbacy of St Martin at Tours where he died in 804.

His writings were many and varied. Over 300 of his letters still survive and he wrote the biographies of several saints (including that of his kinsman, the missionary Willibrord), a number of poems, including one on the history of the church at York, and educational treatises in which he urged both churchmen and freemen to promote learning and establish schools throughout the kingdom. His own teaching methods were largely catechetical: students memorised set questions and answers he prepared on topical subjects and on lessons drawn from the arts and the scriptures. Alcuin also wrote a number of biblical commentaries and liturgical works. Indeed, his work on the liturgy formed the basis of the Roman Missal and helped to establish uniformity in the liturgy of the Western Church.

Being so involved with the production of texts, Alcuin is credited with instituting a method of reproducing multiple copies of a text simultaneously: one monk would dictate while eight or ten others wrote. The script (known as Carolingian minuscule) which was developed in the Tours scriptorium under his direction is the antecedent of modern roman type.

Compared with a figure such as Bede, Alcuin has been described as a conservative interpreter of the writings of others, but it was perhaps this very trait which made him the ideal educator. His introduction of Northumbrian learning to continental centres was to have a profound influence on the subsequent history of European literature.

Northumbria in Europe

As a power-house of wealth and learning, the influence of the Northumbrian Church was felt both in the British Isles and in Europe. The Church of Mercia was founded by monks from Lindisfarne in the mid-seventh century. They established a bishopric at Lichfield which, during the eighth century became a centre of power and artistic patronage in its own right. Highly decorated manuscripts and stone crosses, like those still standing at Sandbach in Cheshire and throughout the Derbyshire Peak District, testify to its output at a time when the bishop of Lichfield aspired to the archbishopric of Canterbury. When Nechtan, king of the Picts, wished to convert his people to Christianity, he petitioned Northumbria for missionaries and builders. Ornately carved shrines at St Andrews and Jedburgh demonstrate their influence in the region. Indeed, some of the decorative motifs of the St Andrews shrine are very closely based on those used on the Rothbury Cross. Moreover, relations between Northumbria and Ireland, which had begun in the late sixth century, and led to the establishment of the Northumbrian Church in the early decades of the seventh century, continued to flourish throughout the period. The decoration of manuscripts such as the Book of Mulling, produced in Ireland in the mid-eighth century, which includes the zoomorphic ornament so familiar in the Lindisfarne Gospels, testifies to the continuing cultural contacts.

Northumbrian missionaries were also active on the European mainland. Wilfrid's missionary work in Frisia was continued by his pupil Willibrord, a Northumbrian nobleman who became the archbishop of Frisia in 695. A century later, Alcuin became the master of Charlemagne's court school in Gaul and one of the central figures of Church reform in the region; he had been trained at York under Ecgbert, one of Bede's pupils. His Northumbrian contemporary, Willehad, was the first bishop of Bremen.

As a result of such activities, Northumbrian artefacts were scattered across Europe. The Codex Amiatinus, one of the three bibles produced at Wearmouth-Jarrow, was taken to Rome as a gift for the Pope by the abbot, Ceolfrith, in the early years of the eighth century. The Franks Casket, perhaps intended as a prestigious gift for a high-status person or institution, was carried to Europe, where it remained until the late nineteenth century. The legacy of such works was to be significant. In Belgium, there is the small ivory ('Genoels-Elderen') diptych, decorated with images of the Virgin Mary and Christ, which was produced by continental carvers inspired by Anglo-Saxon work, in the eighth century. For successive generations, chalices and processional crosses, ivories and manuscripts made by the craftsmen of continental Europe were decorated in the distinctive manner introduced by the artists of the Northumbrian Golden Age.

BEDE (c.673-735)

fig.85 - Model of St Paul's Monastery at Jarrow, as it may have been in the time of Bede.
Bede's World, Jarrow, Tyne & Wear.

Bede was one of the most outstanding figures of Northumbria's Golden Age, whose work was to be of lasting importance in this country and throughout Europe. Born on the estate of the monastery of St Peter's at Wearmouth, at the early age of seven he was entrusted to the care of its founder, Benedict Biscop. In about 682 Bede moved to the newly established sister monastery of St Paul's at Jarrow. He was to stay there for the rest of his life, becoming first a deacon and then a priest. His days were spent observing the monastic discipline, but within this framework he found time to devote himself to the learning, teaching and writing for which he is still renowned. Although it seems that Bede never travelled far from home, he had access to a wide variety of manuscripts in the extensive library at the monastery, and many contacts with whom he corresponded in the British Isles and continental Europe.

Bede's writings demonstrate the breadth of his intellectual curiosity, ranging from scriptural commentaries to grammar, chronology, science, poetry and histories of the abbots. However, his most famous work is the Ecclesiastical History of the English People: *influential throughout the Middle Ages, it is still of key importance to our understanding of the early history of the British Isles in the centuries following the end of Roman rule. Bede's preface to the book tells us that he gathered his information from many different sources, using contacts all over England; material was even provided for him from the papal archives in Rome. This ground-breaking work laid the foundations for historical methodology, and Bede has become known as the 'Father of English History'.*

The Ecclesiastical History *was completed in 731 when Bede was in his fifty-ninth year. Its great importance was quickly recognised at home and abroad. For example, an early manuscript copy made in about 737 (the 'Moore Bede', now in Cambridge University Library) is known to have found its way to continental Europe at an early date and by the end of the eighth century it was in the library of Charlemagne's Palace School at Aachen in Germany.*

fig.86 - Scriptorium at a monastery, as reconstructed by English Heritage.

Lindisfarne Priory Museum.

VI

THE END OF AN ERA: THE VIKINGS IN THE NORTH

Viking Disruptions

By the end of the eighth century the kingdom of Northumbria had been seriously weakened by the internecine feuding of the various claimants to the throne. And, while the power and authority of the Church had managed to offset the insecurity caused by the political upheavals to a certain extent, during the ninth century the stability of this institution was also threatened by attacks of Viking raiders from Scandinavia. One of the first of these was made on Lindisfarne in 793 - but not because it was a Christian centre. The practice of establishing monasteries on navigable waterways and prominent headlands to facilitate communications and trade made them natural targets for anyone seeking easy access to plunder, although not all monasteries proved 'easy' to raid. Warned by the attack on Lindisfarne, the monks of Tynemouth were prepared when, the following year, the Vikings tried to raid them. Brandishing swords, the monks fought back, killing one of the leaders and forcing the rest back to their ships which were driven against the rocks and destroyed in a storm; those who reached the shore were slain.

At first, raids like this occurred only sporadically, during the summer months because the main focus of Viking activity in the late eighth and early ninth

fig.87 - The Viking-age cross at Gosforth, Cumbria with the distinctive Scandinavian ring-chain ornament and a number of scenes illustrating events from Scandinavian mythology; 10th century.

centuries was to colonise the islands to the north and west of Scotland. But in 866 a number of Scandinavian raiding parties joined forces and wintered in the south of England. The following spring this army headed north and captured York. An attempt made by the Anglo-Saxons to reclaim it failed; both claimants to the throne were killed and their armies surrendered. A client-king was installed as a tax-collector for the Scandinavians until they returned, in 869, to use York as a base from which to conquer the East Angles (in 870), the Mercians (in 874), and the Picts and Britons of Strathclyde (in 875). In the following year, 876, their leader, Healfdene "shared out the land of the Northumbrians" and they proceeded to farm it (*Anglo-Saxon Chronicle*). Anglo-Saxon Northumbria had become a Viking kingdom.

These events were seen by Anglo-Saxon churchmen (who perhaps had the most to lose) as apocalyptic events heralding the end of the world. In the *Anglo-Saxon Chronicle* (a history of the period written in the form of annual entries), the attack on Lindisfarne was described as the culmination of a series of portentous events: great flashes of lightning, fiery dragons flying in the sky and famine. In Lindisfarne itself the Viking raids were regarded in the same way. A small grave-stone from the monastery shows a band of Viking warriors on one side and a number of images symbolising the Day of Judgement on the other (*fig.88*). Here the Vikings represent the "wars and rumours of wars" mentioned in the Bible (*Matthew* 24. 6) as one of signs of the end of the world.

Certainly the raids were disruptive. Hoards of coins and precious artefacts were buried in the hope that they could be recovered after the Vikings had passed by (*fig.89*). And, once Healfdene had shared out the land of Northumbria the large estates of the Church and ruling elite ceased to exist. Place-names show that they were divided up among a number of individuals. The lands around Hovingham, in North Yorkshire, for example, had been part of a large and very rich ecclesiastical estate. The ninth century shrine, carved with images of Christ and the Virgin Mary, which was housed in the church at Hovingham was possibly the focus of a local saint's cult attracting pilgrims to the centre. Under the Vikings the landed estates of this rich church were divided up and redistributed among men with names like Frithi (Fryton), Eymundr and Slengr (Amotherby and Slingsby), Brandr and Styrr (Brandsby and Stearsby).

Such redistribution of wealth clearly destroyed the economic basis of the Church and its means of patronage. Manuscripts, after all, need animal skins, and animals need land for grazing; the manufacture of jewellery and church plate requires secure access to gems and precious metals; stone buildings and sculpture depend on quarries, the ability to transport stone, and labour freed from agricultural production; education needs a settled environment with a ready

fig.88 - Gravemarker from Lindisfarne, Northumberland, carved with a band of Viking warriors on one side and a symbolic representation of the Day of Judgement on the other; late 9th century.

Lindisfarne Priory Museum.

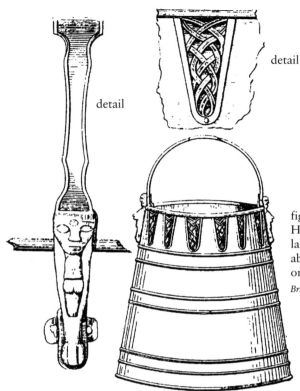

detail

detail

fig.89 - 8th-century bucket found at Hexham, which had been buried with a large hoard of coins in the 9th century, about the time of the Scandinavian raids on the area.

British Museum.

supply of teachers, students, and equipment. With no monastic estates, there were no workshops, libraries and schools able to produce the scholars and high-quality artefacts definitive of the Golden Age of Northumbria.

The Viking Kingdom of Northumbria

What replaced the ecclesiastical economic basis of Anglo-Saxon Northumbria, however, was a kingdom in touch with the far-flung reaches of the Scandinavian world; it was part of vast trade network stretching from the Indian sub-continent and Russia to North America. As part of this world its capital, York (or Jorvik as it was called), became an urban centre on a scale not known since the disintegration of the Roman Empire. A moneyed economy evolved. With the removal of power and wealth from the Church into the hands of individuals, patronage of the arts was taken over by secular landlords - increasingly so during the tenth century as the Scandinavian settlers converted to Christianity (a sure sign that the Church was not totally destroyed by the Vikings).

At Kirkdale, in North Yorkshire, a Scandinavian named Orm rebuilt the church which had fallen into disrepair and set up, over the entrance, a dedication stone recording his work. At Gosforth in Cumbria, a number of impressive stone carvings were commissioned by a local magnate (*fig.87*). In the production of such monuments the art of Northumbria received fresh inspiration from the decorative motifs traditional to the art of the Vikings.

The round or circular form of the cross-head was a feature introduced to Northumbria by the Vikings through their contact with such monuments in Ireland. The 'hogback' (*fig.90*), an entirely new monument form, was developed. Reminiscent of houses with shingle roofs, and sometimes set with beasts at the gable-ends, these monuments may have been inspired by house-shaped reliquaries which formed part of the loot acquired by the Vikings during their raids on ecclesiastical centres. The distinctive ring-chain which fills the lower part of the cross shaft at Gosforth was inspired by similar motifs found on Viking metalwork, as were the long, ribbon-like animals with curved snouts and long 'pigtails' which feature on numerous Viking-age monuments in the area. Scenes from Scandinavian legend and mythology were also used to decorate the sculpture, and in some cases they were set alongside Christian images (as at Gosforth), in attempts to elucidate Christian doctrine in terms which would be appreciated by a Scandinavian audience. Secular figures, warriors and hunters, were also portrayed on the Viking-age commemorative monuments. The effect of the Scandinavian settlement on the arts of Northumbria was one of expanding horizons and renewed experimentation.

fig.90 - A Viking-age 'hogback' from Brompton in Allerton, North Yorkshire; 10th century. *Durham Cathedral Dormitory Museum.*

VII

THE LEGACY OF THE GOLDEN AGE

Cultural Inspirations

The Golden Age of Northumbria did not simply influence the art and learning of early Medieval Europe; its legacy informs almost every aspect of modern life. It laid the foundations of the English language, of English literature, and of English ecclesiastical organisation. Its products continue to inspire today's artists and writers. Modern sculptors use the motifs and forms of the High Crosses in their own creations; poets such as Jorge Luis Borges and Tony Harrison have used the Northumbrian Golden Age and the creativity of its artists to highlight the moral and cultural 'dark ages' of the modern world. Film-makers employ replicas of Northumbrian Anglo-Saxon manuscripts, metalwork and sculpture as touchstones in their recreations of early Medieval settings. The ornate scripts of Northumbrian manuscripts fill advertising bill-boards and shop signs. War memorials and funerary monuments in cemeteries and public squares and parks throughout the world replicate the Northumbrian cross-shafts. Churches are filled with stained-glass windows, hangings, altar-cloths and furniture decorated with the motifs of Northumbrian art.

fig.91 - *The Grammar of Ornament* by Owen Jones (1856), plate LXIV. This influential source book inspired many Victorian designers. The chapter 'Celtic Ornament' illustrates Anglo-Saxon as well as Celtic styles.

Where to Go and What to See

Many of the original buildings and artefacts relating to the Northumbrian Golden Age can still be found in museums, libraries and churches including those listed below.

MUSEUMS AND LIBRARIES:

Alnwick, Northumberland: Castle and Museum

Barnard Castle, Co. Durham: The Bowes Museum

Carlisle, Cumbria: Tullie House Museum and Art Gallery

Chester-le-Street, Co. Durham: Anker's House Museum

Chesters, Northumberland: Clayton Collection Museum

Darlington, Co. Durham: Edward Pease Public Library and Art Gallery

Dumfries, Dumfries & Galloway: Dumfries Museum

Durham: Durham Cathedral Library, Treasury and Dormitory Museum; Fulling Mill Museum

Edinburgh, Lothian: National Museum of Scotland

Hartlepool, Cleveland: Museum of Hartlepool

Hull, Humberside: Hull and East Riding Museum

Hutton le Hole, North Yorkshire: Ryedale Folk Museum

Ilkley, West Yorkshire: Museum

Iona, Argyll: Iona Abbey Museum

Jarrow, Tyne & Wear: Bede's World

Leeds, West Yorkshire: Leeds City Museum

Lindisfarne, Northumberland: Lindisfarne Priory Museum

London: British Museum, British Library, Victoria and Albert Museum

Newcastle upon Tyne: Museum of Antiquities

Otley, West Yorkshire: Otley Museum

Oxford: Ashmolean Museum, Bodleian Library

Scunthorpe, Humberside: Scunthorpe Museum and Art Gallery

South Shields, Tyne & Wear: Arbeia Roman Fort, excavations and museum

Sunderland, Tyne & Wear: Sunderland Museum and Art Gallery

Whitby, North Yorkshire: Whitby Abbey Centre, Whitby Museum

Whithorn, Dumfries & Galloway: Whithorn Priory Museum and excavated site

York, North Yorkshire: York Castle Museum, Jorvik Viking Centre, Yorkshire Museum

fig.92 - Anglo-Saxon Church of St Andrew at Bywell, Northumberland.

CHURCHES:

Abercorn, Lothian: Parish Church (sculpture)

Auckland South Church, Co. Durham: Church of St Andrew (sculpture)

Aycliffe, Co. Durham: Church of St Andrew (Viking-age sculpture)

Bamburgh, Northumberland: Church of St Aidan (original foundation by Aidan; site of his death; Saxon sundial in crypt)

Bedlington, Northumberland: Church of St Cuthbert (sculpture)

Beverley, Humberside: Beverley Minster (bishop's throne; window glass)

Bewcastle, Cumbria: Church of St Cuthbert (Anglo-Saxon cross)

Billingham, Cleveland: Church of St Cuthbert (eighth-century church with ninth-century tower)

Birtley, Tyne & Wear: Church of St Giles (sculpture)

Bolam, Northumberland: Church of St Andrew (late Saxon tower)

Bywell, Northumberland: Churches of St Andrew (late Saxon tower) and St Peter (Saxon nave, north wall and chancel)

Chester-le-Street, Co. Durham: Church of St Mary & St Cuthbert (founded 883 on earlier Roman site by Cuthbert Community; Anchorite Cell houses sculpture)

Collingham, North Yorkshire: Church of St Oswald (sculpture)

Corbridge, Northumberland: Church of St Andrew (Roman arch reused by Anglo-Saxons)

Croft-on-Tees, North Yorkshire: Church of St Peter (Anglo-Saxon cross-shaft)

Dewsbury, West Yorkshire: Church of All Saints (sculpture)

Durham: Durham Cathedral (tombs of Bede and Cuthbert, Cuthbert relics in Treasury; Anglo-Saxon sculpture in Monks' Dormitory)

Edlingham, Northumberland: Church of St John the Baptist (Saxon foundations and west wall)

Egglescliffe, Cleveland: Church of John the Baptist (fragments of Anglo-Saxon stonework in porch)

Escomb, Co. Durham: Church of John the Evangelist (complete seventh-century Anglo-Saxon church; sculpture)

Gosforth, Cumbria: Church of St Mary (Viking-Age cross, sculpture)

Halton, Lancashire: Church (cross-shaft in church-yard, fragments in church tower)

Hart, Cleveland: Church of St Mary Magdalene (remains of Anglo-Saxon church; sculpture)

Heddon on the Wall, Northumberland: Church of St Andrew (partial Anglo-Saxon remains in the fabric of the church)

Hexham, Northumberland: Hexham Abbey (foundations of Wilfrid's church; crypt; Anglo-Saxon sculpture; bishop's throne)

Hovingham, North Yorkshire: Church of St Mary (Late Saxon tower and fabric; Anglo-Saxon shrine front; Viking-age sculpture)

fig.93 - Tynemouth Priory on the site of the Anglo-Saxon monastery.
English Heritage.

Heysham, Lancashire: Church of St Patrick (sculpture; ruins of Anglo-Saxon church)

Ilkley, West Yorkshire: Church of All Saints (cross-shafts in church, fragments in museum next to church)

Irton, Cumbria: Church of St Paul (Anglo-Saxon cross)

Jarrow, Tyne & Wear: Church of St Paul (foundations of Biscop's church; chancel was seventh-century chapel; sculpture; monastic site)

Jedburgh, Borders: Jedburgh Abbey (Anglo-Saxon sculpture)

Kirkdale, North Yorkshire: Minster Church of St Gregory (Anglo-Saxon church restored in Viking-age; dedication stone with sundial; sculpture)

Lastingham, North Yorkshire: Church of St Mary (Anglo-Saxon door jambs)

Ledsham, North Yorkshire: Church of All Saints (Anglo-Saxon tower, walls, imposts, chancel-arch, windows, sculpture)

Leeds, West Yorkshire: Church of St Peter (tenth-century Viking-age cross-shaft)

Lichfield, Staffordshire: Lichfield Cathedral (The Lichfield Gospels)

Masham, North Yorkshire: Church of St Mary (Anglo-Saxon carved column, sculpture)

Middleton, North Yorkshire: Church of St Andrew (sculpture)

Monkwearmouth, Sunderland, Tyne & Wear: Church of St Peter (tower, south and west walls of Benedict Biscop's church; sculpture)

Norham, Northumberland: Church of St Cuthbert (sculpture)

Norton, Cleveland: Church of St Mary (late Anglo-Saxon cruciform church with central tower)

Nunburnholme, Humberside: Church of St James (cross-shaft fragments)

Otley, West Yorkshire: Church of All Saints (sculpture)

Ovingham, Northumberland: Church of St Mary the Virgin (late Saxon tower; sculpture; Celtic stone head)

Ripon, North Yorkshire: Ripon Cathedral (Wilfrid's crypt; Viking-age sculpture)

Rothbury, Northumberland: Church of All Saints (font is base of Anglo-Saxon cross)

Ruthwell, Dumfries & Galloway: Parish Church (Anglo-Saxon cross)

Seaham, Co. Durham: Church of St Mary the Virgin (nave similar to Escomb, possibly seventh-century)

Simonburn, Northumberland: Church of St Mungo (sculpture)

Sockburn, Co. Durham: Church of All Saints (late Anglo-Saxon nave; Viking-age sculpture)

Staindrop, Co. Durham: Church of St Mary (building fabric; sculpture)

Tynemouth, Tyne & Wear: Tynemouth Priory (site of Anglo-Saxon monastery; some worn cross-shaft fragments)

Warden, Northumberland: Church of St Michael (late Anglo-Saxon tower; sculpture)

Wearmouth: see Monkwearmouth

Whalley, Lancashire: Church of St Mary (sculpture)

Whitby, North Yorkshire: Whitby Abbey (site of early monastery; sculpture in Visitors' Centre)

York, North Yorkshire: York Minster (Foundations and Treasury)

OTHER SITES OF INTEREST:

Bamburgh, Northumberland: Bamburgh Castle, the site of British and Anglo-Saxon centres

Birdoswald, Cumbria: Roman fort

Doon Hill, Lothian: British site taken over by Anglo-Saxons

Heavenfield, Northumberland: site of battle between Oswald and Cadwalla, 634

Inner Farne, Farne Islands, Northumberland: site of Cuthbert's retreat

Ladyswell, Holystone, Northumberland: site of one of Paulinus' mass baptisms

Pittington Church, Hallgarth, Co. Durham: twelfth-century paintings of the life of St Cuthbert

Wallington Hall, Northumberland: Pre-Raphaelite paintings of the history of Anglo-Saxon Northumbria

Yeavering, Northumberland: site of the royal centre of the Anglo-Saxon kings

Further Reading

ROMAN BRITAIN:

For general historical introductions, see:

P. Salway & J. Blair, *Roman and Anglo-Saxon Britain* (The Oxford History of Britain, vol.1), Oxford University Press 1984

S. Johnson, *Later Roman Britain*, Granada Books 1980

For books on the art and archaeology of Roman Britain, see:

G. de la Bédoyère, *The Finds of Roman Britain*, Batsford 1989

Shire Archaeology books on: *The Gods of Roman Britain, The Towns of Roman Britain, Villages in Roman Britain, Roman Military Tombstones, Romano-British Wall Painting, Romano-British Mosaics*

G. de la Bédoyère, *Roman Towns in Britain*, English Heritage, Batsford 1992

S. Johnson, *Hadrian's Wall*, English Heritage, Batsford 1989

J. Crow, *Housesteads*, English Heritage, Batsford 1995

C. Thomas, *Christianity in Roman Britain to AD 500*, Batsford 1981

ANGLO-SAXON ENGLAND:

Translations of works by Anglo-Saxon writers:

Bede, *The Ecclesiastical History of the English Nation*, Penguin Classics 1990

Bede, *The Life of St Cuthbert* and *The Lives of the Abbots of Wearmouth and Jarrow,* in *The Age of Bede* (Penguin Classics 1965), which also contains Eddius Stephanus' *Life of Wilfrid*

The Anglo-Saxon Chronicle, edited by G. N. Garmonsway, Everyman Paperback 1994

Alcuin of York (which contains his poem 'On the Saints of the Church of York'), edited by S. Allott, Ebor Press, 1987

Translations of Anglo-Saxon poetry can be found in:

The Earliest English Poems, Penguin Classics 1966

Anglo-Saxon Poetry, edited by S. Bradley, Everyman 1982

The Anglo-Saxon World, an anthology selected by K. Crossley-Holland, Oxford World Classics 1982

Introductory books on the history of the Anglo-Saxons:

F. Stenton, *The Anglo-Saxons*, Oxford University Press 1971

P. Hunter Blair, *The World of Bede*, Cambridge University Press 1970

D. P. Kirby, *The Earliest English Kings*, Unwin Hyman 1991

H. Mayr-Harting, *The Coming of Christianity to Anglo-Saxon England*, Batsford 1972

Books on the archaeology and material culture of the Anglo-Saxons:

D. M. Wilson, *The Anglo-Saxons*, Pelican/Thames & Hudson 1981

M. Welch, *Anglo-Saxon England*, English Heritage, Batsford 1992

B. Yorke, *Kings and Kingdoms of Early Anglo-Saxon England*, Seaby 1990

C. Fell, *Women in Anglo-Saxon England*, British Museum Publications 1984

R. Page, *Life in Anglo-Saxon England*, Batsford 1970

N. Higham, *The Kingdom of Northumbria AD 350-1100*, Alan Sutton 1993

Books on the art of the Anglo-Saxons:

J. Campbell, editor, *The Anglo-Saxons*, Phaidon, 1982

B. Ford, editor, *Early Britain* (The Cambridge Cultural History, vol.1), Cambridge University Press 1988

L. Webster & J. Backhouse, editors, *The Making of England: Anglo-Saxon Art and Culture AD 600-900*, British Museum Publications 1991

D. M. Wilson, *Anglo-Saxon Art, from the Seventh Century to the Norman Conquest*, Thames & Hudson 1984

M. P. Brown, *Anglo-Saxon Manuscripts*, British Library 1991

J. Backhouse, *The Lindisfarne Gospels*, Phaidon 1981 and British Library 1995

J. Lang, *Anglo-Saxon Sculpture*, Shire Archaeology 1988

R. N. Bailey, *England's Earliest Sculptors*, Toronto University Press, forthcoming 1996

THE VIKING-AGE:

For general introductions, see:

H. R. Loyn, *The Vikings in Britain*, Batsford 1977

J. D. Richards, *Viking Age England*, English Heritage, Batsford 1991

R. Hall, *Viking Age York*, English Heritage, Batsford 1994

E. Roesdahl, *The Vikings*, Penguin Press 1991

For books on the art of Viking-age England, see:

R. N. Bailey, *Viking Age Sculpture in Northern England*, Collins 1980

J. Graham-Campell & D. Kidd, *The Vikings*, British Museum Publications 1980

E. Roesdahl, editor, *The Vikings in England*, The Anglo-Danish Viking Project 1981

fig.94 - Stone animal-head terminal, 8th-early 9th century; possibly the finial of a chair end. *St Peter's Church, Monkwearmouth, Tyne & Wear.*

Illustration Acknowledgements

We are most grateful to all the organisations and individuals who have so kindly given permission for their photographs and drawings to be reproduced in this book.

fig.1.   Tyne & Wear Museums. Photographer - Les Golding

fig.2.   The British Library

fig.3.   English Heritage Photographic Library

fig.4.   Tyne & Wear Museums (Archaeology Department)

fig.5.   The Dean and Chapter of Durham

fig.6.   The Trustees of the British Museum

fig.7.   English Heritage Photographic Library.

fig.8.   Kingston upon Hull City Council

fig.9.   Lindsay Allason-Jones

fig.10.   The Dean and Chapter of York. Photographer - Jim Kershaw

fig.11.   English Heritage: Corbridge Museum

fig.12.   The Trustees of the British Museum

fig.13.   The Trustees of the National Museums of Scotland 1996

fig.14.   Jane Hawkes

fig.15.   Museum of Antiquities of the University and Society of Antiquaries of Newcastle upon Tyne

fig.16.   Museum of Antiquities of the University and Society of Antiquaries of Newcastle upon Tyne

fig.17.   The Trustees of the British Museum

fig.18.   Cleveland Archaeology Section

fig.19.   The Trustees of the British Museum

fig.20.   Bede's World, Jarrow. Artist - Terry Ball

fig.21.   West Heslerton Parish Project. Artist - Paul Birbeck

fig.22.   Cecil M.Yuill Ltd, Hartlepool

fig.23.   Museum of Antiquities of the University and Society of Antiquaries of Newcastle upon Tyne

fig.24.   West Heslerton Parish Project

fig.25.   Museum of Antiquities of the University and Society of Antiquaries of Newcastle upon Tyne

fig.26.   Tyne & Wear Museums (Archaeology Department)

fig.27.   Tyne & Wear Museums (Archaeology Department)

fig.28.   Museum of Antiquities of the University and Society of Antiquaries of Newcastle upon Tyne

fig.29.   Tyne & Wear Museums (Archaeology Department)

fig.67. The Trustees of the National Museums of Scotland 1996

fig.68. The Director of the Biblioteca Medicea Laurenziana, Florence, Italy

fig.69. The Director of the Biblioteca Medicea Laurenziana, Florence, Italy

fig.70. The Trustees of the British Museum

fig.71. The Director of the Biblioteca Medicea Laurenziana, Florence, Italy

fig.72. The British Library

fig.73. The British Library

fig.74. The British Library

fig.75. The British Library

fig.76. The British Library

fig.77. Clive Hart

fig.78. Clive Hart

fig.79. The Trustees of the British Museum

fig.80. Jane Hawkes

fig.81. Museum of Antiquities of the University and the Society of Antiquaries of Newcastle upon Tyne

fig.82. Jane Hawkes

fig.83. Jane Hawkes

fig.84. Clive Hart

fig.85. Bede's World, Jarrow

fig.86. Tyne & Wear Museums. Photographer - Les Golding

fig.87. Clive Hart

fig.88. English Heritage Photographic Library

fig.89. Tyne & Wear Museums (Archaeology Department).

fig.90. The Dean and Chapter of Durham

fig.91. P2 ColourLab, Newcastle upon Tyne

fig.92. Tyne & Wear Museums. Photographer - Les Golding

fig.93. English Heritage Photographic Library

fig.94. Tyne & Wear Museums. Photographer - Les Golding

Also published by Sandhill Press

As a complement to the activities of Sandhill Press, you can also visit The Book House at 17 Castle Street, Warkworth where we provide a busy and popular bargain bookshop.

Quality books on all subjects are substantially reduced, most at least half price.

We also stock local books and our own Sandhill Press titles.

Tel: (01665) 712483   Fax: (01665) 713004